"America is blessed with many great [shooters, and over] the years Julie Golob has proved herself to be one of those few. Certainly her skills and her fearless ability to push them to their limits speak for themselves. More important perhaps is her willingness to reach out to the larger community of shooters, especially women, and give them the benefits of those skills. That is the nature of true mastery."

—Michael Bane,
Host of *Shooting Gallery* on Outdoor Channel

"As a veteran of the Smith & Wesson Shooting Team, Julie is one of the most accomplished and respected competitors in the world of shooting sports. As CEO of Smith & Wesson, I have come to respect her superior skill and her true passion and reverence for the sport. Today, people across our country are entering the world of firearms in unprecedented numbers, for purposes of both personal protection and sport shooting. In her new book *Shoot* Julie delivers outstanding expertise and advice, providing readers with the rare opportunity to learn from a true master."

—Michael Golden,
CEO, Smith & Wesson Holding Corp.

"Now I've got one simple answer for all the people asking me how to get started in competition shooting: Get Julie's book. It's everything you need to know to start shooting safely, plus the tips and training that will improve your scores, from the world's most successful female pro shooter."

—Jim Scoutten,
Host of *Shooting USA* on Outdoor Channel

"I've seen many shooters come and go over my career, and Julie stands out as a champion. When all is said and done, Julie, will be one of, if not *the* most winning shooters of all time. She not only has the natural talent, but the drive and discipline to put in the work, day in, day out, year after year to reach her personal goals. And on top of that, she's a wonderful person, a great ambassador, and a positive influence and role model for anyone interested in the shooting sports."

—Rob Leatham,
Multi-National and World Action Shooting Champion

"Having collaborated with many of our top competitive shooters and coaches, I can think of no one who is better qualified to write a current book on shooting sports than Julie Golob. As a former U.S. Army Marksmanship Unit team member, world champion, and current Smith & Wesson team captain, she has spent most of her life walking the walk as a winning competitor, trainer, and ambassador of our sport. Veteran and beginning shooters alike are in for a treat with Julie's new book *Shoot*."

—Chip Lohman,
Managing Editor, *Shooting Sports USA* magazine

"Julie Golob has set the standard for women in the shooting sports. She defines excellence and is what every female athlete should strive to be."

—Maggie Reese, National Multi-Gun Champion and
Top Shot Season 2 contestant on History Channel

"Julie's easy-to-read style comes from her years of hands-on personal experience as an international-level competitor—it's obvious she's comfortable with shooting and teaching. Her tips, techniques, and explanations demystify those pesky questions that new, and even experienced, shooters often have. *Shoot* is a delight to read and a must-have addition to any shooter's library."

—Roy Huntington, Editor,
American Handgunner magazine

"As a professional shooter, I am in constant contact with many of the world's greatest competitive shooters. I have known Julie Golob for many years, on and off the range. Her marksmanship abilities, combined with her knowledge of the shooting sports, are unmatched."

—Doug Koenig,
Multi-National and World Action Shooting Champion

"*Shoot* is a great book on today's shooting sports that will move you on your way to winning that top award. Whether you're a new shooter looking for information or a seasoned competitor, you'll find this book a must-read and a great addition to your shooting library."

—Scott Warren, FBI Hostage Rescue Team and
Multi-National Shooting Champion

"Julie Golob brings years of firsthand experience as one of the top shots in the world of competitive shooting to this fun, easy-to-read overview of the gear, skills, and mindset required to improve your performance, whether you're a beginning shooter or a veteran of sanctioned competitions."

—Andrew McKean, Executive Editor,
Outdoor Life magazine

"Julie's dedication to tackle and conquer as many shooting sports and disciplines as she can has made her one of the most well-rounded champion shooters of all time. This book reflects the excellence she defines."

—Kippi Leatham, Multi-National Shooting Champion and Founder of WomenofUSPSA.com and HerHandgun.com

"I've had the unique opportunity to watch Julie transform from promising contender, to national champion, to shooting icon. This book represents the next logical step in her brilliant career. I highly recommend to anyone interested in the shooting sports that they take the opportunity to benefit from the invaluable wisdom that Julie has accumulated over the past 20 years, and the experience earned in hundreds of hard-fought competitions, thousands of earnest days training, and millions of aimed shots downrange. In *Shoot* Julie has set the standard—you are the shooter on deck!"

—Jay Christy,
U.S. Army Shooting Team, and Triple Canopy Vice-President

"Anyone serious about shooting and the related competition skills will be wise to follow Julie Golob's advice and recommendations. Her skill with firearms speaks for itself, and the details in her book are easy to understand for both novice and professional."

—Ken Hackathorn,
Small arms trainer and consultant

SHOOT

SHOOT
YOUR GUIDE TO SHOOTING AND COMPETITION

Julie Golob
Foreword by **Sandy Froman**

Skyhorse Publishing

Copyright © 2012 by Julie Golob

Foreword copyright © 2012 by Sandy Froman

All Rights Reserved. No part of this book may be reproduced in any manner without the express written consent of the publisher, except in the case of brief excerpts in critical reviews or articles. All inquiries should be addresses to Skyhorse Publishing, 307 West 36th Street, 11th Floor, New York, NY 10018.

Skyhorse Publishing books may be purchased in bulk at special discounts for sales promotion, corporate gifts, fund-raising, or educational purposes. Special editions can also be created to specifications. For details, contact the Special Sales Department, Skyhorse Publishing, 307 West 36th Street, 11th Floor, New York, NY 10018 or info@skyhorsepublishing.com.

www.skyhorsepublishing.com

10 9 8 7 6 5 4 3 2 1

Library of Congress Cataloging-in-Publication Data

Golob, Julie.
 Shoot : your guide to shooting and competition / Julie Golob ; foreword by Sandra Froman.
     p. cm.
 Includes index.
 ISBN 978-1-61608-698-5
 1. Shooting. 2. Shooting contests. I. Title.
 GV1153.G65 2011
 799.3'1--dc23
                    2011037921

Printed in China

To all those who carry firearms in the line of duty to keep us safe.

CONTENTS »

» *Foreword by Sandy Froman*	XIII
» *Preface*	XVII
» *Acknowledgments*	XXI
» *Introduction*	XXIII

Chapter 1 »	SAFETY	1
Chapter 2 »	WHY SHOOT?	8
Chapter 3 »	WOMEN & SHOOTING	11
Chapter 4 »	THE 4-1-1 ON GUNS	16
Chapter 5 »	NRA PRECISION SPORTS	38
Chapter 6 »	OLYMPIC SHOOTING SPORTS	65
Chapter 7 »	SHOTGUN SPORTS	83
Chapter 8 »	HANDGUN ACTION SHOOTING SPORTS	91
Chapter 9 »	MULTI-GUN	136
Chapter 10 »	NOSTALGIA SHOOTING SPORTS	143
Chapter 11 »	TAKING THE PLUNGE	149
Chapter 12 »	FUNDAMENTALS	157
Chapter 13 »	ADVANCED SKILLS	183
Chapter 14 »	PRACTICE ON THE RANGE	223
Chapter 15 »	FROM NEWBIE TO CHAMPION	233

FOREWORD »

Whoever said, "Those who can, do; those who can't, teach" never met Julie Golob. Julie can do both—indeed, she excels at both. Those who have followed Julie's amazing competition shooting career know that she is a champion shooter. With the publication of this book, everyone will know that Julie is also a champion teacher.

I first met Julie in 2005, just six months into my first term as NRA President, when I was invited to attend a women's shooting camp at Gunsite Academy in Arizona. I had trained at Gunsite starting in the early 1980s when Col. Jeff Cooper owned and ran the school, and when you risked ridicule if you showed up with anything on your hip other than a classic, military-style Model 1911 .45 caliber pistol. By the time I met Julie, Gunsite's owner was successful businessman Buz Mills, also a Model 1911 aficionado, but one who recognized that one size (of pistol) does not fit all. He offered firearms training for law-abiding, peaceable civilians through various courses with experienced instructors who helped students choose the best firearm for their particular needs.

The camp's purpose was to introduce women to the sport of action shooting, using female instructors exclusively. Julie was one, along with Lisa Munson and Kay Miculek, all three experienced competition shooters. Although I'd been shooting pistols for many years, my NRA duties didn't allow sufficient time for the training necessary to be competitive in the sport. But I couldn't pass up the opportunity to train with such accomplished sportswomen.

As the course got underway, what impressed me most about Julie was her ability, on demand, to bring all her concentration and focus to the task at hand. We'd be on a break, standing around loading magazines and exchanging stories. Julie would be listening and smiling, showing a perfectly manicured student how to push that last round into the magazine, and then the range master would call us to the line. In an instant, Julie was all business: studying the students, correcting someone's stance, checking another's gear, and verifying up and down the line that there were no fingers on triggers until it was safe. She had a heightened sense of awareness of everything going on around her. I'm sure this is one of the qualities that make her a fierce competitor.

My favorite part of the class was watching the instructors shoot. Watching Julie was a lesson in relativity that would have made Albert Einstein proud. The stopwatch proved how fast she was, but my eyes and my brain recorded what she did as slow motion. Why did it look slow when it was actually fast?

The reason is something my late husband Bruce Nelson, a founding member of the International Practical Shooting Confederation, taught me: in shooting, "smooth is fast." You can't shoot fast enough to make up for wasted motion. Just as the shortest distance between two points is a straight line, the *fastest* distance between your firearm and the target is a straight line. Any time your handgun spends wandering "out of bounds" is time wasted. Julie didn't waste any time. Her smooth presentation to the target made it look slow and effortless, but she was blindingly fast.

It was a pleasure and a privilege to be one of Julie's students. I learned a lot, not just about shooting but about myself. I think I understand better now why it was imperative to learn to shoot and be prepared to defend myself.

One of the best things Julie does in her book is explain why it is important for people, especially women, to familiarize themselves with firearms and, if at all possible, to learn to shoot. Learning to use a gun safely and responsibly is one of the few sporting skills that could someday save your life or the life of a loved one. Learning to swim is another potentially lifesaving skill. Learning to play golf is not!

I've watched thousands of women learn how to shoot. Plenty are seniors, or petite in stature; many have debilitating arthritis or other medical conditions that make it difficult for them to handle a particular firearm—for example, some cannot rack the slide on a full-size semiauto handgun. But these variables pale in comparison to the will of the woman who wants to learn. There's always a different gun that is a better "fit" for such women, or a particular way of loading and unloading the firearm using principles of leverage. Experienced firearms instructors know there are many ways to overcome physical obstacles. Anyone who wants to acquire the skill to shoot can do it. And Julie's book can help show them how.

As NRA Past President, I hope that everyone reading this book will join the NRA if they do not belong already. When people hear "NRA" they immediately think of political issues. But the NRA is first and foremost about firearms training and safety. The NRA was founded in 1871, in the aftermath of the Civil War, by Union officers concerned about the poor marksmanship of Union soldiers. By comparison, Confederate troops were often country boys who had grown up shooting squirrels for the stew pot, thereby honing their marksmanship skills. After the war, Union officers feared that if the newly reunited States were invaded by a foreign power, we would not be able to defend her. So they formed NRA to teach shooting to young civilian men who might later be called to serve their country.

It was not until the mid-1970s that NRA developed its political arm, the NRA Institute for Legislative Action (ILA). NRA would have likely been content to stay out of politics had it not been for the growing national anti-gun sentiment that followed the assassinations of JFK, Martin Luther King, and Robert Kennedy. The push for gun control was on, and the NRA found it necessary to develop political muscle in order to keep its training and competitive shooting programs intact. NRA's political clout today is second to none. We support candidates who support the Second Amendment, regardless of political party. And the reason for NRA's political engagement is to make sure that we all preserve our Second Amendment right to keep and bear arms, whether for self-defense, competition, hunting, recreation, or collecting.

The late NRA board member David Caplan always said: "A right not exercised is a right that ceases to exist." The Second Amendment is the insurance policy on the rest of the Bill of Rights. If we want the Second Amendment to remain vital, we must exercise that right. We should take up shooting, and Julie's book will tell even the novice shooter where to start. Any of us can begin a lifelong enjoyment of the shooting sports with what's in this book.

As Thomas Jefferson wrote in a letter to his nephew:

> A strong body makes the mind strong. As to the species of exercise, I advise the gun. While this gives moderate exercise to the body, it gives boldness, enterprize, and independance [sic] to the mind. Games played with the ball and others of that nature, are too violent for the body and stamp no character on the mind. Let your gun therefore be your constant companion of your walks.

Since she was a young lady tagging along with her dad to the range, Julie has let her gun be her constant companion. And her joy and success in the sport are obvious for all to see. As I write this, Julie Golob has just made history by winning the Ladies Revolver Championship at the USPSA Nationals, making her the only shooter, male or female, ever to win a national championship in all six USPSA divisions (Open, Limited, L10, Production, Single Stack, and Revolver). All I can say in admiration of this remarkable young woman is "Go Julie!"

—Sandy Froman
Tucson, Arizona
September 2011

PREFACE »

My first exposure to the shooting sports was as a child. I would go to the range with my father, mostly because I bickered with my brother and sister. I am the middle child and was often viewed as the "instigator." At first I thought of this arrangement as a punishment, but after a day at the range, my dad and I would enjoy a hamburger and fries on the way home. Dad and I started to bond, talking about a number of different things and listening to music along the way. What I had thought of as punishment actually became fun.

At the range I was something of an anomaly. There weren't very many young girls hanging around. It was mostly a guy place with a handful of women at best. The first matches I went to were silhouette matches. Competitors shot rows of steel targets shaped like chickens, pigs, turkeys, and rams. I liked watching these matches because I could always tell who was doing well, and I enjoyed the light plinking sound the plates made before they fell. I also found it fun to help people clean up the range, picking up the spent brass casings after everyone completed firing.

One day at one of these matches my dad asked me if I'd be willing to spot for him. Spotting is a term used in shooting where someone acts as a coach, letting the shooter know where the bullets impact downrange. This information can help a shooter make necessary changes to their sights to ensure they hit the targets. I was game and being naturally competitive I liked the idea of helping dad perform well. Instead of just sitting there, watching my dad shoot and picking up some brass, I had a role. From that moment on, I was more than just a kid at the range. We were a team.

The partnership continued as I began to attend other matches. I was ten years old and working prestigious events in United States Practical Shooting Association (USPSA) competitions. I did anything, from helping clean up the range to pasting targets, even serving as a scorekeeper and range officer at some competitions. Working as a range officer and volunteering at the range helped me to learn the rules of the sport and also gave me a great understanding of sportsmanship.

By the time I was fourteen my dad and I decided that I was ready to give shooting a try. Up until that point I wasn't physically strong enough to work the controls on my dad's handguns, but by the time I was a teenager I was both physically and mentally ready. All the years of volunteering, watching top women shooters in action, inspired me. Women like Kippi Leatham, Kay Miculek, and Sharon Zaffiro were talented and fierce competitors, yet still stopped to sign autographs and offer a smile on the range. I also had the huge benefit of being able to shoot local monthly matches with Sheila Brey, the first woman ever to make master class in USPSA. Watching Sheila shoot, seeing how respected she was as a competitor, by both men and women alike, made me realize I wanted to begin competing.

I started out slow. When I say slow I mean *really* slow, in a sport that stresses speed. I focused on shooting as many center hits as possible, often posting the highest raw target score of anyone in our local events. I really liked that. With that competitive streak, I constantly wanted to do better and I became more aggressive in competition, striving to go faster and faster. My dad never pushed me or made me shoot. He wanted me to enjoy it. The only thing he always stressed was safety, so that when I was ready to take my shooting to the next level I had a firm foundation of good, safe shooting skills.

I attended my first national championship as a junior in high school in 1994, hitching a ride with my shooting hero, Sheila Brey. At the event I caught the eye of the United States Army Marksmanship Unit's (USAMU) Action Shooting Team coach. I was beyond thrilled, and my parents completely supported my decision to join the Army Shooting Team.

I wish I could say the same for many of my teachers and even the principal at my school. In New York State in the 1990s, with strict gun laws and a political administration with a gun control agenda, not many were interested in supporting my goals. I was also a straight A student, graduating high in my class. No one could understand why I wanted to join the military and pass up scholarships and college. I was told at one point that I was wasting my life, and that if I wanted to join the Army, the only option I should consider was looking into West Point to become an officer. It was hard, but I ignored all the negative comments. I knew that in the Army I would make a living and at the very least, if shooting didn't work out, I had the opportunity to take advantage of tuition programs and pursue other opportunities.

I left for basic training in July 1995 and competed for the USAMU for nearly eight years. I was able to dedicate nearly every day to improving my shooting, and accumulated many titles, including being named U.S. Army Female Athlete of the Year in 1999. When I made the decision to leave the Army, I realized that I wanted to make a career in the firearms industry and work to promote shooting sports in any way that I could. I took a position working for Glock, Inc.'s Sport Shooting Foundation. A couple of years later, an opportunity to work for Smith & Wesson came up, and I jumped at the chance to be the captain of their successful shooting team, accumulate even more titles, and to spread the word about shooting sports and my passion for competing.

I was very fortunate to have a father who was interested in shooting and one who didn't think the sport was just for boys. For those who have no exposure to shooting, it is very easy to think that shooting sports aren't necessary or even valid. This is a sport that people from all walks of life enjoy. I have always enjoyed writing, and this book is yet another way for me to get the word out. I want this book to be the introduction for someone who may not have had a parent or family member in his or her life who could expose them to safe, fun shooting competitions.

In a perfect world, everyone would be open-minded about shooting. At the very least though, I would love to see everyone learn and understand firearms safety, regardless of whether they want to shoot or not. After that, an understanding that shooting sports are safe and enjoyable might help change negative preconceived notions about guns and how people use them.

ACKNOWLEDGMENTS »

My journey as a competition shooter began with two people. To my mom and dad, thank you for never letting me think that shooting and hunting were just for boys, for never stifling my competitive spirit, and for always believing in me.

Writing has always been something of a hobby for me, but until I was approached by Bill Bowers at a firearms industry trade show, I had never seriously considered writing a book. As I entertained the idea and made the decision to give it a shot (pun intended), Bill not only became my literary agent, providing help and insight on the publishing world, but also a good friend. To Bill and his wife, Eileen, thank you so much.

Thank you to Tony Lyons and Skyhorse Publishing for giving me the opportunity to share my passion for shooting sports with the world.

A special thank you to Sandy Froman, a woman I look up to as a leader and spokesperson for the National Rifle Association, for taking the time in her extremely busy schedule to write the foreword for this book.

I have been inspired by and blessed to have shared shooting with so many special people. A special thank you to all my "IPSC aunts and uncles" from my days as a junior competitor, Rob and Kippi Leatham, "Coach" Ray Arredondo, Jay Christy, and Jerry and Kay Miculek.

Many of the firearms, shooting sports gear, and ammunition images in this book have been provided by my generous sponsors. Thank you to Smith & Wesson, Benelli, Warren Tactical Sights, ASYM Ammunition, Federal Premium Ammunition, Rudy Project

Eyewear, Safariland, VihtaVuori Powders, Starline Brass, Próis, and Action Target.

The incredibly talented Yamil Sued shot most of the photos in this book. Yamil's eye for shooting both a camera and a gun makes him one of the most sought-after photographers in the industry. Thank you for your time and talent, my friend.

Thank you also to the NRA, USA Shooting, U.S. Army Marksmanship Unit Public Affairs, Scott Carnahan, Chip Lohman, and Stephen McKelvain for providing additional photos. Those featured in images throughout the book represent remarkable individuals in the shooting sports, from junior competitors Rachael Crow and Janae Sarabia, to event volunteers, to respected champions Sherri Jo Gallagher, Jim Henderson, Doug Koenig, Rob Leatham, Kenda Lenseigne, Jerry Miculek, Maggie Reese, Kim Rhode, Michael Voigt, and members of the U.S. Army Marksmanship Unit and Armed Forces Shooting Teams.

Two very special people provided graphics and editing assistance: my brother Bill Goloski and dear friend Lois Chase. You both are amazing technical artists and I can't thank you enough for your time and skills.

Bill also spent many hours designing the front and back covers of the book. Thanks so much, Bill. I love it!

Finally, thank you to my husband. Simon, you have put up with many "what do you think of this and thats" and late nights. Your insight as an excellent shooter and experienced instructor, and your technical knowledge, have been invaluable. Thank you for your support and love.

INTRODUCTION »

Welcome to the world of shooting! This book is designed to serve as both a guide for new shooters and as a useful resource for people who already shoot. The most important consideration when looking into learning how to shoot a firearm or compete in a shooting sport is to ensure that you know how to handle firearms safely. There can be no compromises when it comes to being safe with firearms. Even if you are a seasoned competitor or own firearms, I encourage you to read the chapter on safe gun handling, Chapter 1, Safety. This chapter also addresses eye and ear protection standards, as well as precautions you should take to limit lead exposure.

If you aren't an enthusiast, you might ask yourself, why shoot? As I like to say, why not? Chapter 2, Why Shoot? covers the different reasons why people choose to start shooting and how it becomes a pastime they love. Chapter 3, Women & Shooting specifically addresses concerns that women may have in getting started. Because shooting is still a predominantly male sport, this information might be helpful to women who may be reluctant to give shooting a try. If you are already an enthusiast or competitor, you may wish to breeze through this material. After all, you've already caught the shooting bug!

Another portion for those new to guns is Chapter 4, The 4-1-1 on Guns. Here I cover general firearms information for those who are completely new to shooting. This chapter starts with understanding how ammunition works and also covers the different types of modern firearms. This information can be very helpful if you are looking to purchase a firearm. Keep in mind that some guns are ideal for certain types of competitions. An understanding of the differences, types of actions, and how ammunition is loaded can help you decide what gun is suitable for a specific division or competition you might be interested in. This book is by no means a technical manual. Instead, the goal is to explain in simple terms how different firearms function.

Next we explore the different shooting sports. Shooting sports are organized into types, including the precision-based sports of the National Rifle Association (NRA), Olympic sports, shotgun sports, handgun action shooting sports, multi-gun competitions, and nostalgia shooting sports. Details for each sport and the guns and gear required to compete are explained for each. Keep in mind that there are plenty of shooting sports that didn't make it into the pages of this book. New sports are forming frequently, and rules for existing shooting sports change.

Once you have an idea of the different shooting sports, you can then make a plan to give one (or more) a try. The final chapters of the book address how to take the plunge, the fundamentals, advanced skills, how to practice efficiently, and how to evolve from a new shooter to a champion. Whether you decide to pursue shooting as a fun hobby or develop the skills to become a distinguished shooter, these chapters will provide insight into how to attain your competition goals.

Chapter 1 »

SAFETY

Safety is the most critical component in any shooting sport. Shooting competitions are often considered to be "extreme" sports because there is a certain level of risk involved. Competitors are, after all, shooting live ammunition! It is absolutely necessary at all times to stress safety on the range, and safety precautions must always be taken.

Competitions and organizations have very strict rules when it comes to handling firearms. Regardless of whether you decide to give a shooting sport a try or not, everyone should know the cardinal rules of firearms safety:

1. **Treat all firearms as if they are loaded**. What if you know that your gun is unloaded? It doesn't matter. If you treat a firearm as if it is loaded, you greatly reduce the likelihood of shooting something you don't intend to.
2. **Keep your finger off the trigger and outside the trigger guard until you are ready to shoot.** One tip to achieve this is to keep your trigger finger straight and off the trigger until you are acquiring your target. This helps eliminate any startle reflexes that might cause you to press the trigger when you do not wish to.

3. **Do not point at or cover anything with the muzzle you do not intend to shoot.** The muzzle is what we call the "business end" of a gun. Anytime you point or aim a firearm, you are making a very important statement, indicating that you are preparing to shoot. That means you are willing to put a bullet into whatever you are pointing at. There is nothing casual about safe gun handling.
4. **Be certain of your line of fire and backstop.** Basically this means that if you are shooting at a target, it is your responsibility to know where your bullets will impact. Shooting ranges should be set up so that rounds impact in a safe area, like a hill or berm. If you aren't sure, don't shoot.

Knowing and applying these fundamental rules will improve your safe gun handling skills. Keep in mind that there are also sport- and range-specific safety rules. At many events and ranges, handling firearms is prohibited except under the direct supervision and instruction of a range or safety officer. The majority of ranges are also "cold" ranges. A cold range means that firearms are to remain unloaded at all times until you receive commands from a range officer to handle and load ammunition into your firearm. "Hot" ranges are those that allow shooters to carry a loaded firearm on their person.

> **TIP:** *If you are legally carrying a loaded firearm onto a cold range, immediately seek out a match official or safety officer and ask them what the procedure is for unloading your firearm in order to comply with the range or competition rules.*

Safety gear is also required for all shooters and spectators when they are on the range. The basics are eye and ear protection. Eyesight and hearing protection are not areas to skimp and try to save money. When considering eye protection, you should look for minimum protection standards. The American National Standards Institute (ANSI) has established impact ratings to use as guidelines for eye protection. There is a good chance your favorite designer shades might not be ANSI rated. It's best to have a dedicated pair of glasses to use when you are shooting. Look for glasses that have an ANSI rating of Z87+. Consider selecting wraparound frames and those with lenses that provide ample coverage around your eyes to reduce the chance of injury.

Dirt, target debris, and even the oil from a firearm can hit your eyes if they are not protected. Splatter is a common term for fragments of the bullet that ricochet off steel targets. Oftentimes splatter can be so small you can't see it, but it tends to be very sharp. *Never* shoot at steel targets without proper eye protection. A good rule of thumb is to put on your safety glasses whenever you step foot onto a range.

Make sure that any eye protection you wear on the range meets ANSI ratings. Companies like Rudy Project make suitable eye protection that is also fashionable.

TIP: *Shooting glasses can come in a wide variety of tints based on the sports. Some allow for targets and sights to appear to be brighter. Clear lenses are the ideal initial investment for most shooting sports.*

Two types of common hearing protection for shooters are earmuffs and earplugs. Earmuffs cover the ears, while earplugs are inserted into the ears to block out noise. Loose earmuffs simply don't do the job. They should fit tightly yet comfortably on your head, with no gaps in the seal around your ears. Some manufacturers even offer electronic muffs that block out sharp noises like gunfire but amplify sounds like start buzzers and speech so you can easily hear what's going on around you.

With earplugs there are several different options. At the least expensive end of the spectrum, foam earplugs can be inserted into the ears to block out noise. There are also harder, plastic versions as well. Another option is a set of custom earplugs. These plugs are molded directly into the user's ear for a personalized fit. Finally, there are even electronic molded earplugs that work similarly to the electronic earmuffs mentioned above.

Pictured above are three types of hearing protection, molded ear plugs, foam ear plugs, and earmuffs, which help protect hearing while shooting firearms.

One thing to keep in mind when selecting hearing protection is the Noise Reduction Rating (NRR). By law, every hearing protection product sold in the United States must have an NRR. It's simple. The higher the NRR, the better the protection.

> **TIP:** *I often wear double hearing protection when I shoot—both earplugs and earmuffs—to protect my hearing. As an added benefit, double hearing protection helps reduce the natural reaction people can have to loud noises, often dubbed "flinch."*

Lead Poisoning

One safety concern that is often overlooked is protection from exposure to lead and other contaminants. Lead and other particles are released into the air after a shot is fired. In some cases this dust can even be seen surrounding a shooter in what appears to be a smoke or haze. Outdoor ranges pose less risk than the confined spaces of indoor ranges. Lead particles, inhaled or ingested over time, can eventually lead to poisoning.

Lead poisoning is serious business, and the symptoms are often not apparent until the level of lead in the blood is very high. It's a good idea to have your lead levels regularly checked by your physician. This is even more important if you shoot at indoor ranges, where ventilation can be an issue. Checking for lead involves a simple blood test. Your doctor can help you analyze your results to make sure you stay within safe limits.

Ways to reduce exposure to lead on the range:
- Wash your hands and face with cold water, soap, or D-Lead, a cleaner designed to remove arsenic, cadmium, chromium, lead, mercury, silver, and zinc from skin and other washable surfaces when you are finished at the range.
- Avoid touching your eyes, nose, and mouth on the range.

- Avoid eating or drinking on the range, but if necessary, be sure to wash your hands and face before handling any food or drink.
- Shower as soon as you get home from the range.
- Keep your shooting clothes, shoes, and gear separate from your other apparel.

If you have young children at home, it is especially important to follow the last two points above. Lead is particularly dangerous to children, and they are more easily affected than adults.

Pregnant women should also avoid lead exposure. According to Fabrice Czarnecki, MD, MA, MPH, FACOEM—who also serves as Director of Medical-Legal Research at The Gables Group, Inc.; Chairman of the Police Physicians Section of the International Association of Chiefs of Police; and Vice-Chair of the Public Safety Section of the American College of Occupational and Environmental Medicine—there are significant risks involved for women who shoot while pregnant.

Dr. Czarnecki says: "Pregnant women should avoid lead exposure. Lead exposure during pregnancy is associated with serious complications for both the fetus and the mother, including miscarriage. Children who were exposed to lead before they were born may have lower IQ and impaired mental development. Even at low levels, lead exposure has been associated with preterm delivery, congenital abnormalities, and decreased birth weight. Current research suggests that there is no safe lead exposure threshold for children, infants, or fetuses."

He even warns about lead for women who are breastfeeding. "Lead is transmitted from the mother to the fetus, and is excreted in breast milk. For women who are breastfeeding, it is best to avoid unprotected firearms training. Wearing an appropriate respirator and careful hand hygiene should allow most breastfeeding women to safely train with firearms, especially if using lead-free ammunition."

Other hazards for pregnant women include cleaning solvents and noise. The chemicals in solvents used for cleaning firearms can be toxic to an unborn child. "Noise exposure during pregnancy has been associated, in human studies, with several adverse outcomes, including miscarriage, intrauterine growth retardation, preterm delivery, hearing loss in babies and children, and hypertension in pregnancy.

"I recommend that, during pregnancy, women not shoot firearms at all, unless in self-defense," Dr. Czarnecki adds.

Being safe on the range involves more than just firearms safety rules. Proper eye and ear protection should be worn at all times to reduce the risk of injury. With simple steps, shooters can also prevent lead poisoning and exposure to airborne contaminants. Remember, safety is always your first priority!

Chapter 2 »

WHY SHOOT?

Many people have a fear of firearms. Because guns can be dangerous in the wrong hands, some people wish to avoid them altogether. Learning how firearms work and what they are capable of can help those who have a fear of them. There is a huge amount of bad information about guns in the media and on the Internet. Exaggerated reporting by liberal media, anti-gun groups, and dramatization on television and movie screens can create a false sense of what shooting is really like—that it's all dangerous and results in someone getting hurt. Despite tens of millions of gun owners in the United States, guns are sensationalized. It is as the saying goes: knowledge is power.

Even if you have no interest in owning a firearm, shooting one, or competing in a shooting sport, having knowledge of proper firearm safety can help you deal with firearms in various situations in the best way possible.

Shooting can be empowering. It can build a great sense of accomplishment and confidence. The controlled skills that are required in order to hit targets successfully, whether you're looking to drill the center of a bull's-eye target, bust a clay target flying through the air, or compete in an action-packed, fast-paced sport like action shooting, where you are required not only to shoot at targets, but do so while moving, can make you feel self-assured and confident.

Many of you who are reading this book may already own a firearm. You may hunt or carry a firearm for self-defense and are looking for ways to improve your gun handling skills. Shooting sports give you the opportunity to handle your firearms on a more frequent basis. When competing actively, you simply use your gun more, which then increases your ability both to shoot and manipulate its controls.

In addition to taking a hunter safety course in order to become a hunter in most states, you might want to consider engaging in a shooting sport with the firearm that you use for hunting. This is going to help you gain confidence for when you do need to make a shot on an animal. With all my experience in competition, I know my limitations as a shooter and I have a solid foundation of successful shooting to feel confident taking a shot on game.

Many people purchase firearms for defensive purposes but never think about how they would handle them in these situations. For those who have firearms for self-defense, either on their person or in the home, participating in a shooting sport will also keep you active and familiar with your firearm.

Perhaps you were active in sports in high school and college. The rigors of life have left you with no real options to rekindle that competitive nature you once had. The shooting sports can give you an opportunity to compete on a consistent basis. Depending on what you feel comfortable with, you can choose sports based on how physically demanding they are, to reignite that competitive spark.

Finally the shooting sports are simply a blast—pun intended. It doesn't just come down to the shooting and competing, though. The people, from competitors to volunteers, are some of the best you will ever meet. Chances are if you show up to your first match unprepared, a number of people will offer you their own gear to help make your experience pleasurable. Shooters want more shooters to participate. Unsportsmanlike conduct is not tolerated, and safety is stressed at all times. The goal is for everyone to have fun.

These are just some of the reasons why people shoot. Whether you have a practical mindset for learning how to use a firearm for protection or just wish to get involved in a sport that will challenge you, there are plenty of shooting sports out there you can try.

Chapter 3 »

WOMEN & SHOOTING

Guns and shooting in general have traditionally been for men. Despite equal rights, prescribed gender roles still thrive in today's society, and there are still some who think only certain careers and certain sports are suitable for women. I couldn't disagree more.

> **Firearms safety is something everyone should know and understand.**
> **Shooting sports are for both men and women.**

Women can enjoy and be just as successful in shooting sports as men. In fact, many shooting sports focus on skills that have no basis in strength or size. The ability to align sights on a target and squeeze the trigger has nothing to do with gender.

I know women from all walks of life who love to shoot. Doctors, lawyers, members of the press, housewives, and more all enjoy shooting firearms as a hobby or carrying them for personal protection. The bottom line is that there is really no stereotype for the shooter or gun owner.

Many women might feel reluctant to keep firearms in the home or to begin competing in a shooting sport because they have children. As someone who grew up in a house with guns and as a

Shooting is not just a sport for guys, and more and more women are taking up shooting sports, including Rachael Crow (left) and Janae Sarabia (right), two junior champions who are turning heads and taking names in competition.

mother myself, I know there are ways both to own firearms and to ensure that your children are safe. The NRA has a wonderful program called the Eddie Eagle GunSafe Program that lays the foundation for what children should do when they come across a firearm. Teaching children how to handle situations can help them to deal with them safely. The learning points are "Stop! Don't Touch. Leave the area. Tell an adult." Keeping firearms locked up is another way to ensure that firearms are inaccessible to children and other inappropriate individuals. Firearms ownership is a responsibility not to be taken lightly.

Because shooting and competing with firearms have been historically male-dominated activities, getting started as a woman might be intimidating for some. A quick Internet search for videos of women shooting can yield some saddening and disappointing results. Some videos feature a woman who is given no instruction on fundamental

The NRA's Eddie Eagle Program teaches children about gun avoidance and is geared to pre-K through third grade. For more information about this program, visit www.nrahq.org/safety/eddie. Photo courtesy of the NRA.

shooting skills and handed a large-caliber handgun with significant recoil. The result: the woman is startled and sometimes even laughed at. This type of video is disturbing on many levels, especially when simple steps could have been taken to make shooting a pleasurable experience instead of a negative one.

For every negative video or poor "instructor" there are those who successfully teach women not just to shoot, but also to shoot very well. There are plenty of women-only programs out there if you want to get started and want to do so with other ladies. The NRA has an excellent program called Women on Target, and there are plenty of individual courses that offer instruction for women by women. That's not to rule out instruction by men, but many women find that they are more comfortable learning from an experienced woman. Additional information about Women on Target can be found at the NRA's website at www.nrahq.org/women/isc.

The National Shooting Sports Foundation's First Shots program is another that welcomes women. In addition to learning about firearms safety and local gun laws, participants have the opportunity to take their first shots on target with the help and guidance of a certified instructor. Because all participants are novices, the experience is tailored to make sure everyone is comfortable. For more information about the First Shots Program, visit www.firstshots.org

Regardless of who teaches you to shoot, I do have a few woman-specific tips to help you with your journey.

- Wear double hearing protection, both earplugs and earmuffs. Women can be sensitive to loud noises. Using double hearing protection can reduce the impact the sound of gunfire has on your ability to align your sights and squeeze the trigger.
- Consider starting with a rimfire (.22 caliber) firearm. The minimal recoil will allow you to focus on learning the fundamentals without the distraction of how the gun kicks. If you do shoot a centerfire first, try to start with reduced-power ammunition and a small caliber like 9mm.
- Use a strong grip when firing, especially when firing your first shots with a firearm. Controlling the firearm's recoil will help you feel more confident, and you can always adjust your grip accordingly with subsequent shots.
- Use your body to help you control recoil. The more aggressive you are in your stance, the better. Bending at the knees and waist with the feet more than shoulder-width apart while leaning into the gun will allow you to use your body to absorb the impact of the recoil. It may feel exaggerated, but you can always adjust to a less aggressive stance later. For a detailed description and photos on stance see Chapter 12, Fundamentals.
- Research gear and accessories that could improve your shooting. An example of this is the use of drop and offset holsters in many action shooting sports. This type of holster allows the gun to sit lower on the body, similar to where a holster would sit for a male

competitor. The offset feature allows the gun to remain straight up and down without canting in toward the curve at the waist, allowing for a faster draw.

When considering gear or firearms designed for women or those with features that are desirable to women, seek out as much information as possible. Some guns and gear are simply offered in a "feminine" color and offer no benefit. Others implement features that make shooting easier for women with shorter arms, smaller hands, and less upper body strength than men. Many Benelli long guns offer ComforTech Systems on their stocks, an easy and quick way to adjust the length of pull. A shorter length of pull for a woman with shorter arms than a man can make all the difference in being able to fire a shotgun or rifle comfortably. The Smith & Wesson M&P pistol comes with three interchangeable back straps—small, medium, and large. The small grip allows women with smaller hands to fully reach the trigger and magazine release button efficiently. All of these are steps in the right direction, and as more and more women get involved in owning firearms and in shooting sports, we can expect to see modifications and improvements continue.

Chapter 4 »

THE 4-1-1 ON GUNS

👆 **LINGO:** *Bullet, Ammo, Cartridge, Round, Shells = common words used to describe ammunition*

The first step to understanding modern firearms is learning how a bullet works. It's easiest to start with describing the components of a typical handgun or rifle cartridge. There are four basic components to a cartridge. The first is what people refer to as a case, shell, or piece of brass. Cases can be made of a variety of materials, such as steel, aluminum, and brass (hence the common name). Think of a case as a jar. It is essentially a tube specifically sized to the caliber of the firearm. One end is open. The bottom is closed and is referred to as the case head. In centerfire

A piece of brass or case is the component of a bullet that holds the primer, gunpowder, and projectile.

ammunition, the case head has a depression with a tiny hole in its center called the primer pocket.

> ◉ **TIP:** *Bullet caliber generally corresponds to the diameter of the inside of a firearm's barrel. Before loading any ammunition, make sure the caliber matches the gun.*

A primer is a very small explosive that sits in the primer pocket. It has two purposes. It serves to ignite the gunpowder, and also plugs the hole in the bottom of the case. The case is filled with a very specific amount of gunpowder called a powder charge. There are many types of gunpowder. Some types burn quickly and others slowly. Ammunition manufacturers use specific measurements for gunpowder, to the tenth of a grain, much as a cook would follow a recipe in baking.

Finally, a bullet or projectile serves as a cap for the cartridge. There are many types of bullet designs. Just some of the various names for bullets are: full metal jacket (FMJ), plated, lead, hollow-point, roundnose, wadcutter, hardball, soft tip, shot, tracer, and green tip. Each type has a specific purpose and performs differently,

Primers are small explosives that ignite gunpowder in the cartridge.

Gunpowder, primers, and brass make up the bottom portion of a cartridge.

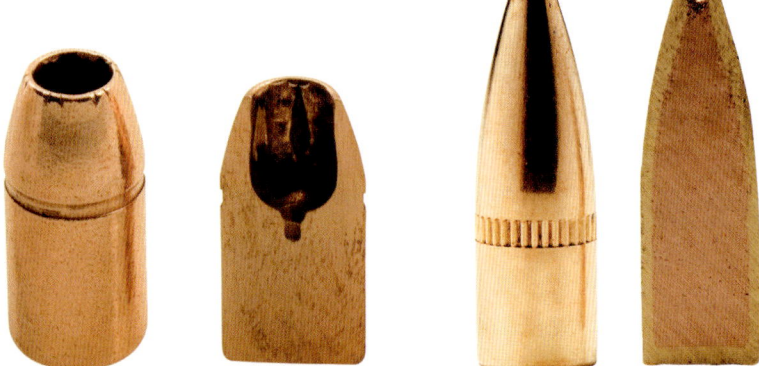

Bullets, like the pistol (left) and rifle (right) pictured here serve as the projectile portion of a loaded cartridge.

from projectiles that break up on impact to those that are designed to pass through dense mediums.

When a gun is loaded and ready to fire, the cartridge lies in position, ready for action. Once the trigger is pressed a series of internal mechanical movements take place, resulting in the firing pin or hammer striking the primer. When struck, the primer explodes, with the energy traveling through the tiny hole in the primer pocket. This explosion ignites the gunpowder inside the case. Pressure builds inside the case until the bullet is forced out of the case and through the barrel. The shot is fired.

In modern firearms the two basic types of ammunition are rimfire and centerfire. In the example outlined above, centerfire cartridges have a primer resting in a primer pocket centered in the back of the case. Rimfire cartridges, typified by the .22 LR (long rifle)

The photo above shows both centerfire (left) and rimfire (right) ammunition. With the centerfire case, the firing pin or striker has struck the center of the case where the primer sits. In the spent rimfire case, you can see where the firing pin or striker has struck the rim of the case.

 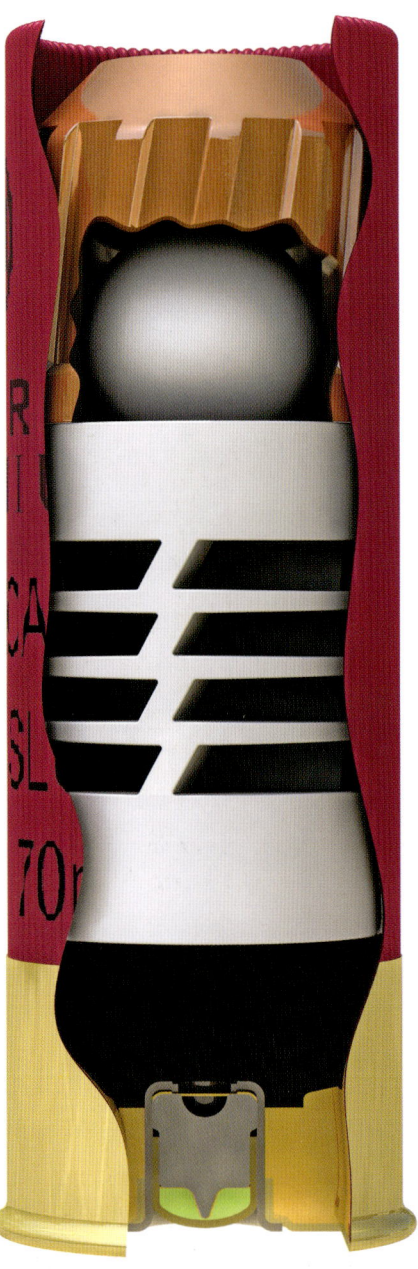

Some shotgun ammunition is designed to fire multiple pellets whereas others are designed to fire one large slug as shown by these cutaway images provided by Federal Premium Ammunition.

Factory ammunition is commercially produced, and loads are designed for specific purposes, like the wide variety of ammunition produced by ASYM Ammunition pictured here.

cartridge, are much smaller in diameter than most centerfire ammunition. Because the case head isn't much larger than the circumference of a primer, the entire back end of rimfire ammo is designed to act like a primer. Instead of striking the center, the firing pin strikes the rim, hence the name rimfire ammunition.

Shotgun ammunition can either fire a number of pellets or one large slug. The type that fires pellets is commonly used for trap or skeet shooting. Slugs are often used in hunting larger game and are sometimes required in fast, action-paced, multi-gun competitions.

In shotgun ammunition the case head is commonly brass with a primer much like centerfire pistol or rifle ammunition. The case body is made of plastic. Powder lies at the bottom of the shell and is kept in place by a plastic wad. The wad separates the gunpowder from the pellets or slug, and the case is sealed at the front end.

There are two ways to buy ammunition. The first is ready-made ammunition you can buy at a store, often called factory ammo. Ammunition companies use specific bullet weights, designs, and gunpowders to create ammo for specific purposes. Some ammo is designed for defensive applications and penetration, while other ammo is geared for target shooting.

The other way to acquire ammo is to make it yourself, a practice called reloading. Many shooters choose to reload their own ammunition to save money. It's kind of like buying a pie at a bakery. If you want pie for dessert, you can go to a pie shop, purchase a ready-made pie, and bring it home. The other option is heading out to the grocery store, buying the entire list of ingredients, and making it yourself. Reloading is definitely more time-consuming, but it does have its benefits. First, it tends be less expensive in the long run because you can purchase components in bulk. The brass portion of the ammo is collected after it has been fired and is the component that can be reloaded. Reloading also allows you to customize ammunition to your guns and purposes.

> **TIP:** *All .22 rimfire ammo and some centerfire ammunition that uses aluminum cases cannot be reloaded.*

Those who reload use specific measurements when making ammo, much as a cook would follow a recipe in baking. Bullet weight, gunpowder measured to the tenth of a grain, how many times brass has been reloaded, and how tightly the case is sealed with a crimp are just some of the concerns that come into play when making ammunition yourself. Reloading can be dangerous if proper procedures are not followed and safety gear like eye protection and latex gloves are not worn. If you plan to reload, understand that though there are benefits, you must be meticulous throughout the entire process.

Did you know that some ammo is more powerful than others? Power factor is the calculation of bullet weight multiplied by the velocity of the bullet when fired, which is then divided by 1,000. Some shooting sports have minimum and maximum ammunition power factors.

Many firearms use magazines to store ammunition. Magazines come in many shapes and sizes and can either attach to a firearm or be integrated into the firearm itself. Revolvers use moon clips or speed loaders, devices that hold rounds in the precise position of a revolver's cylinder to allow for easy loading. There are even speed loaders for shotguns. These are tubelike devices that allow a number of shotshells to be loaded in one motion.

Types of Firearms

There are many types of modern firearms. Manufacturers are constantly researching and developing new guns every year. Some of the most common types are listed below.

Handguns

Handguns are firearms that can be fired and held in one or both hands. Types of handguns include semiautomatic pistols and revolvers. Handguns can be centerfire or rimfire. Revolvers use a cylinder to house ammunition, while semiautos use magazines to feed ammunition into the firearm's chamber.

Semiautomatic Pistol

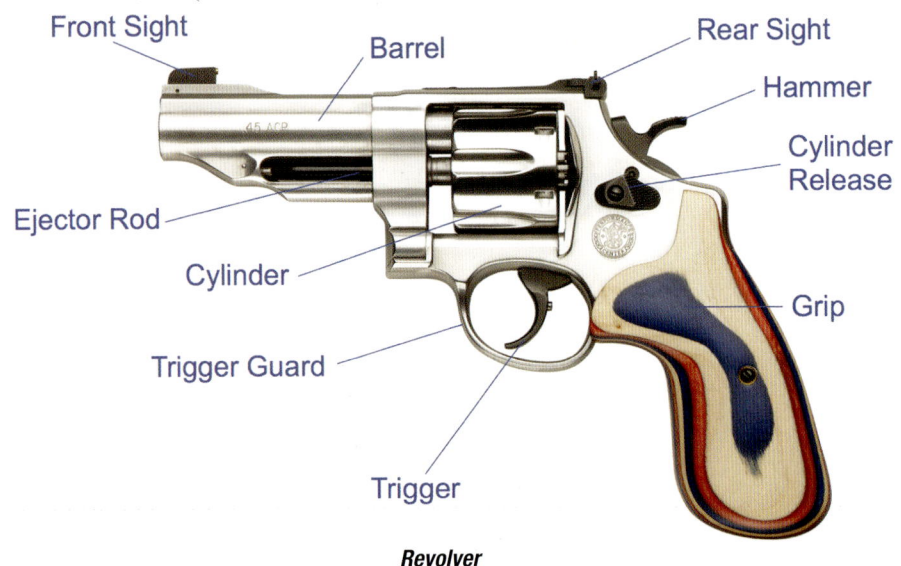

Revolver

Rifles

Rifles are firearms designed to be fired using both hands, from the shoulder. Commonly referred to as long guns, rifles have rifling cuts inside the barrel. Rifling consists of spiral grooves that are cut inside the barrel that cause a bullet to spin, greatly increasing the gun's ability to shoot more accurately at greater distances. Many rifles are capable of shooting projectiles at high velocities. Some common types used in competition include bolt-action and semiautomatic rifles.

Semiautomatic Rifle

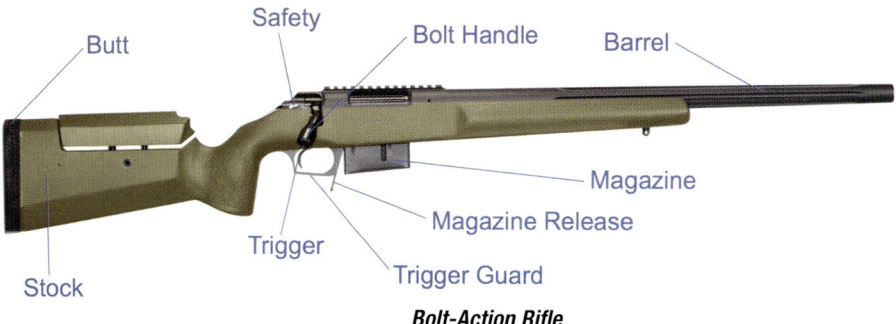

Bolt-Action Rifle

Shotguns

Like rifles, shotguns are long guns that are also fired using both hands and from the shoulder. Unlike rifles, shotguns generally do not have rifling cuts in the barrel. Because of this, shotguns are

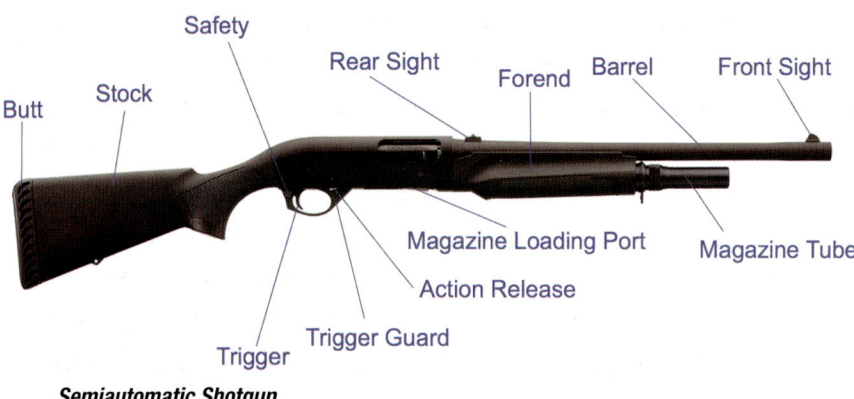

Semiautomatic Shotgun

Pump-Action Shotgun

Side-by-Side Shotgun

Over-and-Under Shotgun

able to fire both single projectiles called "slugs" as well as multiple projectiles, and are also less accurate at distance than rifles. Common types include semiauto, pump action, over-and-under, and side-by-side.

Before the invention of the self-contained cartridge in the 19th century, loading a firearm was a time-consuming process. All the components for a shot—gunpowder, wadding, and ball or bullet—had to be loaded individually. The ignition mechanism (first matchlock, then flintlock, and later a metal percussion cap) had to be arranged at the breech behind the gunpowder, and the hammer cocked to fire the weapon. In the past thirty years, "nostalgic" muzzleloading firearms have enjoyed something of a resurgence in popularity. Many areas have special hunting seasons when only "primitive" firearms are allowed. There are even shooting sports that use muzzleloading firearms exclusively, as detailed in Chapter 10, Nostalgia Shooting Sports.

Firearms Categorized by Loading

Firearms can also be categorized by how ammunition is loaded. As the name indicates, single-shot firearms are designed to hold only one round at a time. There are many different types of single-shot

Single-shot firearms like this Thompson/Center G2 Contender pictured above must be reloaded each time in order to shoot again.

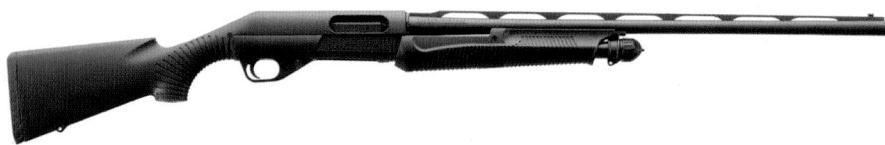

A pump-action shotgun like the Benelli Nova Pump pictured above requires that the shooter pull back and push forward on the forend in order to load a new round.

firearms, from muskets and modern-day muzzleloaders to highly precise centerfire rifles. Take a look at the photo of a Thompson/Center G2 Contender on page 27. This gun features a top break. The shooter places the round into the loading chamber and closes the firearm by lifting up on the bottom of the barrel. After the shot is fired, the shooter pulls down on the barrel to expose the chamber and removes the brass to load the next round.

Other manual feeders include pump and lever actions. Pump-action shotguns are used for both law enforcement and military purposes, as well as some divisions of shooting competitions. In order to eject the spent case and load a new shell, the shooter pulls back and then pushes forward on the forend of the shotgun in a pumping motion.

Lever-action rifles are commonly used in cowboy action shooting sports. These rifles feature a looped lever incorporated underneath the rifle's trigger guard. The shooter pushes down on the lever to eject the brass and pulls back up on the lever to load a fresh round.

Revolvers use a cylinder to hold ammunition. When the trigger is pulled, the cylinder rotates the next round into position. A shooter simply pulls the trigger each time he wishes to fire. Most modern revolvers have cylinders that hold five to eight rounds. Moon clips and speed loaders are used exclusively for revolvers.

The 4-1-1 on Guns

Lever-action rifles are used in some cowboy action competitions. The shooter must pull down and then up on the lever in order to load a round, as shown in the photos above.

A moon clip is a small, thin piece of metal with cutouts to secure the ammunition near the head of the case to allow the shooter to load the cylinder of a revolver in one motion. A revolver's cylinder must be cut to allow for the moon clips in order to use them, though. Speed loaders also allow for loading the cylinder all at once and require no special cuts in the cylinder, but are also bulky in comparison to moon clips. In order to load, the shooter must either push or twist the release to remove the loader from the ammo.

Moon clips and speed loaders are ammunition storage devices used to load revolvers.

Magazines represent another type of loading device that stores and feeds ammunition. Magazines, commonly referred to as "mags," can be either internal or detachable. They generally have four basic components: the magazine tube, base plate, spring, and follower. The magazine tube is what holds the ammunition. The follower is either plastic or metal and cradles the lowermost round. It essentially follows the cartridges up the length of the magazine tube as they are fired. The magazine spring rests below the follower and its job is to push the rounds up the mag. The base plate caps off the bottom of the magazine, holding the spring and follower in place.

Many bolt-action firearms use magazines. Bolt-action firearms represent another type of manually fed firearm. These rifles are commonly used in hunting and precision shooting sports. Many use an internal, fixed magazine, while others feature a detachable magazine. The shooter must activate the bolt handle by pulling back

Magazines like the ones pictured here are ammunition storage devices used to load a variety of firearms.

Bolt-action firearms are common in both hunting and precision rife shooting sports.

to eject the empty case and then pushing forward to feed the next round into position.

Semiauto is the term used to describe magazine-fed firearms that fire one bullet per trigger pull. A semiauto firearm "automatically" executes all steps necessary to prepare the gun to fire again after each shot. The magazine is generally inserted into the grip or bottom portion of the firearm. Once a shot is fired, the gun mechanically ejects the spent brass, and the magazine feeds the next round into position in order for the shooter to keep firing.

Full-auto is the term used to describe types of firearms that function much in the same way as semiautos, except full-autos shoot continuously while the trigger is depressed and are commonly referred to as machine guns. They can be belt-, magazine-, or drum-fed. Some are set up to deliver bursts of fire, like the United States military M16A2 rifle. The M16A2 has a selector switch for semiauto, full auto, and three-round burst.

Types of Actions

Single-action, double-action, and striker-fired are all terms used to describe firearm actions. These terms are also commonly used to describe the functions of the trigger. For beginners and those learning about firearms, describing the way a trigger works according to its type of action is often the best way to begin to learn about them. Instead of going into specifics of how each action works mechanically, a brief introduction of each type based on how the trigger activates either the hammer or striker is outlined in the following pages.

Single Action

With single-action firearms, think of the internal mechanics of the trigger. In order for the gun to fire, a round must be chambered and the action cocked. In some firearms the shooter must reset the trigger by cocking the hammer each time. In others the trigger is automatically reset as part of the series of mechanical events after a shot is fired. Essentially, the trigger's purpose is to release the hammer to strike the primer. Single-action triggers often feature a short distance to pull the trigger and often feel lighter, or easier to pull. A common single-action design is the 1911 pistol designed by John M. Browning.

The Model 1911 pistol was designed by John M. Browning in 1911 and is still a very popular handgun used in shooting sports today.

Double Action

Unlike single-action triggers, the double-action trigger essentially has to pull double duty. Pulling the trigger both cocks and then releases the hammer. The hammer in this type of firearm can either be internal or external. Because of this, the length of pull on a double-action firearm is generally much longer than that of a single-action gun. Think of a double-action trigger as a long, continuous pull from start to finish. A common double-action design is the Smith & Wesson Model 442, a popular concealed-carry handgun also known as a "snub nose" revolver.

A common concealed-carry firearm also used in Back Up Gun divisions in defense-based shooting sports, the Smith & Wesson 442 features a double-action trigger.

Double Action/Single Action (DA/SA)

Just as the name indicates, DA/SA firearms are capable of firing both single and double action. The first pull of this type of action is double action, that longer pull that ends up both cocking and firing the gun. All subsequent shots go into single-action mode, with a lighter trigger feel. DA/SA guns are often chosen for defensive and law enforcement applications. An example of a DA/SA action is the Smith & Wesson Model 5906.

Firearms that feature a double-action first shot with subsequent shots fired in single action, like the Smith & Wesson 5906 pictured above, are often desirable for concealed-carry firearms.

Striker Fired

In single- and double-action firearms, the hammer is responsible for striking the firing pin. In striker-fired guns, there is no hammer. Instead, the striker assembly and the trigger work together to fire the shot. Triggers on striker-fired guns have a unique feel. Unlike most double-action triggers, there is usually a lot of slack when you initially start pressing the trigger. About midway through the pull, the tension builds or feels tighter until the shot breaks. Striker-fired handguns like those in the Smith & Wesson M&P Series are used by both law enforcement agencies and competition shooters.

Regardless how the action works, trigger pull is measured by weight in pounds or grams. Triggers can be described by feel as being crisp or having a lot of roll. The lighter the trigger, the more difficult it is to distinguish the feel. Advanced shooters know exactly what kind of trigger they prefer and are intimately familiar with how and when the shot breaks.

As you can see, there are many of different types of firearms. Most established shooting sports have evolved to account for these types

The Smith & Wesson M&P pistol features a striker-fired action. It is used by competitors and also carried by law enforcement officers on the job.

based on modifications, weight, capacity, and trigger pull. Some sports allow only specific firearms. Other competitions are much more broad but categorize types of firearms into divisions. Take a deep breath! That was a lot of information to process, but you'll find that even this basic knowledge will help you on the next step of this journey.

In the next several chapters, we will explore different shooting sports. Some may appeal to you more than others. The chart below lists shooting sports and color-codes them by type. In most cases, precision shooting sports are stationary events, and these are identified by light blue. Shooters have a time limit to fire a designated number of shots. Accuracy is the focus. Events that require shooters to be precise, using small targets, but are more time-intense, are color coded in green. In these events the targets are moving through the air, available for a short period of time as in clay target shotgun sports, or shooters are timed in their events, as with Biathlon. Action sports are identified by orange. Accuracy is still important, but targets are much larger, and there is a heavy emphasis on speed. In many of these events, both the target and the shooter move.

	Type	Single Firearm sport	Multiple Firearm sport	Highest Level Event (international & U.S.)
NILA Precision	Precision (Time Limit Scoring)	✓ *Exception NRA Conventional Pistol		World & National Championships
Olympic Rifle & Pistol	Precision (Time Limit Scoring)	✓		Olympic & National
Olympic Biathlon	Precision (Time Limit Scoring)	✓		Olympic & National
Shotgun (Olympic & U.S. Sports)	Clay Target	✓	✓	Olympic, World & National
Action Shooting	Speed	✓	✓	World & National Championships
Cowboy Shooting	Speed	✓	✓	World & National Championships

Chapter 5 »

NRA PRECISION SPORTS

You are meticulous and precise in everything you do. You enjoy breaking things down to the most minute of details and are a true "scientist" at heart. Or maybe you think it's just really cool to be able to drill the same hole through a target again and again. If so, you might be a precision shooting sports junkie. I have some good news for you! You have a lot of sports to choose from.

Why so many precision sports? The first shooting sports were precision-based, and competitions today retain some of the same style and even equipment used in those events. The vast majority of precision-based sports are run by the National Rifle Association (NRA). The NRA's National Matches at Camp Perry, Ohio, draw competitors from all over the United States, even internationally. Because the National Matches have strong roots in military marksmanship, service teams from the different branches of the military still compete at Camp Perry today. Most of these NRA sports are precision competitions and cover a full spectrum of guns from pistols to rifles, with shots fired as close as 10 meters in air events to full-bore rifle competitions out to 1,000 yards.

Whether it's shooting a rifle from a single position or firing a course of fire with three different handguns, the goal is the

Sgt. Sherri Jo Gallagher shows that women can not only perform well but they can also dominate in NRA precision events. In 2010 this U.S. Army soldier won the overall High Power National Championships with a score of 2396 out of a perfect 2400, beating the previous record by an incredible 9 points, and all the guys. Photo courtesy of the U.S. Army Marksmanship Unit Public Affairs.

same: shoot as many center hits as possible. In this type of shooting, it all comes down to how you apply the fundamentals of marksmanship from your shooting position. Fire a perfect score and you could instantly become a living legend in the world of shooting.

Five ability classifications are generally used in these shooting sports. The highest classification is the prestigious High Master ranking, followed by Master, Expert, Sharpshooter, and Marksman.

With the exception of NRA Silhouette competitions, shooters in NRA precision events set their sights on bull's-eye targets with the goal of shooting the center on every shot, as shown in this photo of U.S. Army Marksmanship Unit Service Pistol Team member and multinational champion, Jim Henderson. Photo courtesy of the U.S. Army Marksmanship Unit Public Affairs.

Not all NRA events use all five classifications. Some recognize only the bottom four.

The NRA also has many special categories recognized in each sport. Special categories indicate a special level of competition and can be designated for age groups, sex, and even military service. Some of these include senior, grand senior, junior, intermediate junior, sub-junior, police, woman, National Guard, Reserve components, and military veteran. The organization also recognizes team events in specific competitions.

There are specific rules for physically disabled competitors in NRA events. If a competitor is unable to complete a designated course of fire due to a physical handicap, the organization allows for a petition to be filed with the NRA Protest Committee. The petition requires that competitors fully explain their disability, submit photographs, and include a statement from a medical doctor in order to compete with modified equipment or make a change to the course of fire.

The NRA requires that a minimum award schedule be recognized for registered tournaments. In most cases, the winner in each individual match and in each aggregate is acknowledged. The high-scoring competitor in each class (High Master, Master, Expert, Sharpshooter, and Marksman) also receives an award. Team awards are issued according to the rules as well.

For the best of the best, the NRA has a distinguished program for many of their shooting sports. Competitors must be eligible according to the competition rules and must shoot specific qualifying matches in order to accumulate credit points. Credit points are awarded to each event based on the 10 percent of the highest posted scores. Those who reach designated minimums receive the coveted Distinguished Badge for that event. Members of the Armed Forces are authorized to wear a distinguished badge in place of the marksmanship qualification badge on their dress uniforms.

The vast majority of NRA competitions are precision-oriented, with scores based on how close shots land to the center of a target. Many of these competitions mirror international events, specifically those at the Olympic Games. Generally, precision shooting sports involve one or multiple shots on a single target. There are a few exceptions though, like Silhouette competitions and International Rapid Fire, where competitors have more than one target to shoot in a string of fire. Even though Silhouette courses feature steel targets that must fall to score, the distances, precision skills required, and liberal times qualify these as precision events.

To go through each of the NRA's specifics for individual competitions and courses of fire would fill the pages of this book and beyond. And to be honest, it would probably be a bit boring to read. There are often different options for courses of fire that even

This is the Distinguished Badge earned by Jim Henderson, one of the most accomplished pistol shooters at the National Matches at Camp Perry. He has won numerous national titles, as well as the coveted President's Hundred award a record six times. Photo courtesy of Jim Henderson.

In the precision sports, a number of shooters compete at the same time on the firing line as shown in this photo of members of the U.S. Army Marksmanship Unit's Service Rifle Team. Photo courtesy of the U.S. Army Marksmanship Unit Public Affairs.

include reduced distances and smaller targets in the event that ranges cannot accommodate the full distances for all shots. The important thing to know if you're interested in getting involved in any of these sports is that there are specific rules for the firearms that include caliber, firearm weight, overall length, and other modifications. In most cases, muzzle brakes and compensators are prohibited. Specific rules apply for sighting systems like the use of metallic (iron) or telescopic/optic sights. There are also regulations regarding special shooting equipment like gloves, jackets, pants, shoes, spotting scopes, ground mats, cloths or pads, kneeling rolls, "shooting kits," and slings.

⚠ *No exceptions! Even if it's not specifically listed in the rules, it is important to wear proper eye and ear protection when on the range.*

As with any sport, you will want to pay close attention to any penalties associated with specific competitions. Extra hits on targets, misses, and early or late shots are just some examples of where penalties can be issued and affect your overall score. In many cases there are allowable malfunctions and what are referred to as "alibi runs" with very specific scoring procedures. Dry firing may be permitted, but only at specific times within the competition. Sighting shots may be allowed as well, but also vary from sport to sport. Learning the rules for the competition is absolutely critical in order to be successful and enjoy the sport to the fullest.

🖐 **LINGO:** *Where is your ECI? An empty chamber indicator (ECI) is a flaglike device specifically used in NRA competitions. The flag is inserted into the firearm's chamber to indicate that the chamber is indeed clear and safe. You may need an ECI in order to compete in some NRA competitions. The photo shows both an ECI (bottom right) and other devices used by shooters to indicate the gun is unloaded.*

The NRA uses very specific language and range commands. It's a good idea to learn the range commands before starting any competition. Listen and follow all commands, especially those that let you know when you are permitted to handle your firearm and equipment. Here are a few more terms that you can expect to hear at an NRA event:

Cease Fire!—Cease Fire indicates that either the time limit is up and firing has concluded, or it can also be an emergency command where all competitors must stop shooting immediately.

Load—You may load your firearm.

Is the firing line ready? The firing line is ready.—This language is used to ensure that all competitors are ready to commence firing upon the command to begin shooting.

Is all firing completed on the right? Is all firing completed on the left? All firing is completed.—These questions are issued to ensure that all competitors have completed their shots on the firing line. "All firing is completed" is announced before the command to unload.

Unload—Unload your firearm

Is the firing line clear? The firing line is clear.—These commands are issued to indicate that the firing line is clear of loaded firearms.

Following is a list of the NRA's shooting sports with a brief description of important information. You want to make sure that you download a copy of the rule book affiliated with each sport to make sure that you're in compliance with the specific rules for each event. Rule books can be found at www.nrahq.org/compete.

NRA BB Gun

Yes, the NRA has a specific sport for BB guns! If only Ralphie from *A Christmas Story* had known about this program, perhaps his mother would have approved! NRA BB Gun is a true grassroots, entry-level competition for junior competitors. In fact, competitors may compete only up to the calendar year they turn fifteen years old. Shooters use shoulder-held smoothbore BB guns with metallic sights only, which cannot weigh over 6 pounds. Not much can be done to these BB guns, and very few modifications from factory original can be made. Ground cloths, slings, and kneeling rolls are allowed, but other competition-enhancing equipment such as shooting jackets, shoes, trousers, gloves, and compression garments are specifically prohibited. Even the number of sweatshirts a competitor can wear in competition is restricted. The intention is to eliminate an equipment race and keep the sport true to the entry-level competitor and gear.

The BB gun target is a bull's-eye target with a 10 ring of 0.125 inch fired from 5 meters. The positions used in the match are prone, standing, sitting, and kneeling, in that order. There is a course of fire using all four positions as well as a three-position course from prone, standing, and kneeling. Finals are not required but are encouraged in order for shooters to gain competition experience. When used, the finals are similar to Olympic competition format, where competitors fire 10 shots, 60 seconds for each shot (see Chapter 6, Olympic Shooting Sports). National records are recognized for specific courses for both individuals and five-person teams. The classifications used in this sport are Master, Expert, Sharpshooter, and Marksman.

NRA International Style Pistol

The NRA sanctions events that mirror those shot in the Olympics and feature metallic-sight pistols only. For specific details on each of these events refer, to Chapter 6, Olympic Shooting Sports. International targets specific to each sport are used. The NRA also offers reduced course of fire options at reduced distances for these competitions for indoor and limited distance ranges. The NRA uses four classification levels for awards for each of the sports: Master, Expert, Sharpshooter, and Marksman. Below is a brief description of each event in NRA International Style Pistol.

Men's Rapid Fire—An event for .22 caliber pistols. The course of fire is a total of 60 shots divided into two 30-shot portions fired on targets set at 25 meters. As in Olympic Rapid Fire, competitors fire five-shot strings in eight, six, and 4 seconds.

Men's & Women's Center Fire and Sport Pistol—This is divided into two sections, and competitors fire a precision portion of 30 shots consisting of six, five-shot strings with a time limit of five minutes to fire all five shots in each string. The second portion of the event is the rapid-fire portion that involves assuming a ready position and firing one shot in 3 seconds for a total of five shots in the string. The shooter returns to the ready position for a 7-second pause between target presentations. The target distance is 25 meters. Two different targets are used, a precision target and the rapid-fire target. The men shoot centerfire handguns, commonly .32 caliber, and women compete with .22 rimfire. Women's Sport Pistol is a recognized event in the Olympics; the men's centerfire event is not.

Men's Standard Pistol—This is a 60-shot course divided into three 20-shot portions. In the first portion, competitors have 150 seconds to fire five shots, fired in four strings. This is followed by four strings of five shots fired in 20 seconds. The course concludes with four strings of five shots in 10 seconds. All rounds are fired at targets set at 25 meters from the firing line with .22 caliber handguns.

Free Pistol—In another course of fire using .22 caliber handguns, competitors in Free Pistol competition have two hours to fire 60 shots at the International Precision Target set at 50 meters.

Air Pistol—There are separate courses for men and women in Air Pistol. The men's course is 60 shots in one hour and 45 minutes. The women's course is 40 shots fired within one hour and 15 minutes. All shots are fired from 10 meters.

NRA Conventional Pistol

Also commonly referred to as service pistol or Three-Gun, NRA Conventional Pistol is a precision sport featuring .45, 9mm, .22, and .38 Special caliber handguns. Known as service pistol because firearms used are specific service weapons, the U.S. Armed Forces M1911, M1911A1, and M9 pistols. Ammunition is also restricted to rounds manufactured for the U.S. Government ("government-issue") for those competing with service firearms. The sport is not limited to the military, however, and there is the option to compete with non-service handguns with optics. All five classification levels are recognized: High Master, Master, Expert, Sharpshooter, and Marksman.

Conventional Pistol is often referred to as Three-Gun, for pistol shooters because in events like the NRA National Matches in Camp Perry, Ohio, scores are calculated for course-of-fire scores with the .22, centerfire, and .45 caliber handguns. Many shooters compete with three different firearms, but others use the .45 caliber pistol twice, as it qualifies for the centerfire portion of the match.

There are two yard line distances in Conventional Pistol, the 25- and 50-yard lines, with the 10 ring just 3.36 inches in diameter. As with most NRA events, there are several course-of-fire options, but all feature slow, timed, and rapid-fire portions. Slow fire is fired first and at the greatest distance, with ten shots in 10 minutes. Timed fire occurs on the close target range, and shooters fire two strings of five shots in 20 seconds, all on the same target. Rapid-fire is also shot on the short line target and is a total of ten shots, fired in two strings, 10 seconds each.

There are two different divisions within Conventional Pistol: Service and Any.

Service

This is the iron-sight division of Conventional Pistol featuring the U.S. Pistol .45 Caliber (M1911 and M1911A1), the U.S. Pistol 9mm (M9), Distinguished Revolver in .38 Special and Standard Small-bore

.22 caliber pistols. Modifications are limited, and there are specific trigger weights for firearms. Other commercially produced firearms of the same type and caliber are also permitted, but are subject to specific rules. In Excellence-In-Competition matches, ammunition with specific bullet weights must be used.

Any

As the name indicates, any pistol or revolver in centerfire .45 and rimfire .22 may be used. Modifications can be made to these firearms, but specific trigger weights apply. Optics are also allowed.

NRA Precision Air Rifle

The NRA's Precision Air Rifle program combines Olympic air rifle and three-position. Rifles used must be either compressed air or CO_2 rifles of 4.5mm (.177) caliber. Shots are fired on a bull's-eye target with the 10 ring measuring 0.55mm. All shots are fired from 10 meters. Shots are fired from the prone, kneeling, and standing positions specifically in that order. There is a time limit for each shot, 1.5 minutes for each prone and kneeling shot and 2 minutes for each shot in the standing position. As in the precision Olympic sports, finals are reserved for the top eight competitors. Competitors have 75 seconds for each shot in a 10-shot series. National records are recognized for specific courses for both individuals and four-person teams. The classifications used in this sport are Master, Expert, Sharpshooter, and Marksman.

NRA Sporter Air Rifle Position

The NRA's Sporter Air Rifle program is essentially the same as Precision Air Rifle outlined above, with the exception of the equipment used. Think of Sporter Air Rifle as the NRA's grassroots air rifle program, where the compressed air or CO2 rifles cannot exceed 7.5 pounds. Only factory-manufactured internal parts may be used. Externally, just a simple piece of tape or streak of paint may be added to the barrel to reduce glare. Stocks may be modified for length, but must remain factory, and specific rules apply. As in Precision Air Rifle, Master, Expert, Sharpshooter, and Marksman classifications are observed.

NRA Small-bore Rifle

Small-bore Rifle matches feature .22 caliber rimfire rifles, specifically those chambered to use .22 short, .22 long, or .22 long rifle cartridges. The standard rifle has no restriction on barrel length or weight, but does have a minimum trigger pull of 3 pounds. There is also a Light Rifle division that limits the rifle's weight to 8.5 pounds or less and a minimum trigger weight of 2 pounds. For competitors in the Junior Rifle division, any trigger that is deemed safe is allowed, without any trigger pull minimums. Metallic sights and optic sights are both permitted. Four classifications are assigned to NRA Small-bore: Master, Expert, Sharpshooter, and Marksman. The shooting positions used are prone, sitting, kneeling, and standing.

NRA Small-bore Rifle matches have the flexibility to be held either indoors or outdoors, allowing clubs and ranges to account for changing season and range restrictions. Indoor courses use 50- or 75-foot targets, and outdoor courses use targets at 50 yards, 50 meters, and 100 yards, or any combination of these targets and distances. With several course-of-fire options in the sport, the main difference lies in the time allowed per shot. In Indoor Conventional Matches, shooters have one minute each from the prone, sitting, and kneeling positions, and 1.5 minutes from standing for each shot. In Outdoor Prone, Metric Prone, and Position events, one minute is allowed for prone and 1.5 minutes for sitting, kneeling, and standing positions. In Indoor and Outdoor NRA Metric Position Courses, even more time is allotted, with one minute for prone, 1.5 minutes for kneeling, and two minutes for the standing position. There is also a long-range course that features a 200-yard target, but this course is not eligible for classification purposes or for national records. For the outdoor events, personal wind indicators are allowed.

NRA International Style Rifle

The NRA's International Style Rifle rule book is rather intimidating, but it essentially covers different types of precision rifle competitions, ranging from events like 10-meter air rifle to 300-meter competitions with .32 caliber rifles. The smallest target is the 10-meter target, with a 10 ring dot of 0.5mm. The 10 ring gets slowly bigger with the 50-foot target at 0.76 mm, the 50-meter target at roughly 9mm, and finally the 10 ring on the 300-meter target at 1.80 inches. Positions used in these competitions are prone, standing, and kneeling, usually in that order. There are specific weight limits to the rifles used, and some events even have specific minimum trigger weights. Time allotted for each shot is 1.5 minutes each for prone and kneeling and 2 minutes for standing, or an overall time for each specific position within a course. International Style Rifle refers to Small-bore Free Rifle, Small-bore Sport Rifle, 300m Free Rifle, 300m Standard Rifle, and Air Rifle.

Small-bore Free Rifle

This is a competition that uses .22 caliber rimfire rifles. The overall weight of the rifle may not exceed 8 kilograms, and additional firearm modifications and equipment restrictions are listed in the rule book. Courses of fire can be shot either indoors or outdoors and include a 60-shot prone course with targets at 50 meters/50 yards, a 120-shot three-position course at 50 meters/50 yards, and a 120-shot three-position course from 50 feet.

Small-bore Sport Rifle

This is another competition that uses rifles .22 caliber rimfire rifles, and rifle weights cannot exceed 6.5 kilograms with additional firearm modifications and equipment restrictions listed in the rule book. As in Small-bore Free Rifle, courses can be fired either indoors or outdoors and include a 60-shot prone course with targets at 50 meters/50 yards, a 60-shot three-position course with targets at 50 meters/50 yards, and a 60-shot three-position course from 50 feet.

300m Free Rifle

The 300-meter courses in NRA International Style use rifles chambered in .32 caliber with additional firearm modifications and equipment restrictions listed in the rule book. Even though it is called "300 m," courses can be fired from 300 meters, 300 yards, or 200 yards using specific targets for each. There are two courses of fire. The first is a 120-shot three-position course that can also be condensed to a half course of 60 shots. The second is a prone course of with a total of 60 shots.

300m Standard Rifle

Another type of competition using .32 caliber rifles, 300m Standard Rifle also has the requirement of a minimum trigger weight of 1,500 grams, and the overall weight of the rifle cannot exceed 5.5 kilograms. Additional firearm modifications and equipment restrictions are listed in the rule book. The course of fire consists of 60 shots fired from the prone, standing, and kneeling positions at 300 meters/300 yards/200 yards, all within 150 minutes.

Air Rifle

The International Style Air Rifle competition uses compressed air or CO_2 rifles in 4.5 mm caliber with additional modifications and equipment restrictions listed in the rule book. The weight of the air rifle cannot exceed 5.5 kilograms, with additional firearm modifications and equipment restrictions listed in the rule book. All air rifle competition is fired from standing position in either a 40-shot or 60-shot course from 10 meters.

NRA international Full-bore Prone Rifle

The NRA's Full-bore Rifle events use large-caliber rifles at significant distances up to 1,000 yards, with all shots fired from the prone position. Full-bore Prone consists of Target Rifle, International Target

Rifle, and F-class. Additional firearm modifications and equipment restrictions are listed in the rule book. Not only do competitors need skill to shoot their rifles precisely, but because of the target distances in the course of fire, learning how to read the wind and adjust for it is absolutely critical. In fact, because this is so challenging, personal wind indicators and self-contained wind gauges are allowed. Five ability classifications are recognized: High Master, Master, Expert, Sharpshooter, and Marksman.

Target Rifle & International Target Rifle

These competitions use metallic-sight rifles chambered in .308/7.62mm or .223/5.56mm. The main difference between Target Rifle and International Target Rifle lies in minimum trigger weights and overall rifle weight. Target Rifle has no restrictions. International Target Rifle has a minimum trigger weight of 1.5 kilograms (approximately 3 pounds), and the total weight of the rifle cannot exceed 6.5 kilograms (approximately 14 pounds, 5 ounces). Additional firearm modifications and equipment restrictions are listed in the rule book.

Specific targets for the 300-, 500-, and 600-yard lines and a target for shots fired at the 800-, 900-, and 1,000-yard lines. The 300-yard target has the smallest 10 ring at 5.85 inches, and the 10 ring, keeps getting larger the farther the distance, with the 800-, 900-, and 1,000-yard target with a 10 ring of 20 inches. There are both single-stage match courses of fire and also standard multiple-stage, or aggregate match courses of fire. There are both individual and team courses of fire. The individual courses are the full-bore regional individual course consisting of 90 shots, a midrange course with 45 shots, and a national match individual course of 180 shots. The team courses are the prone regional team course of 40 shots and the midrange regional team course of 45 shots. National records are recognized at each yard line.

F-Class Rifle

Another NRA rifle sport featuring extreme accuracy is F-Class. All shots are fired from the prone position, and because the rifle may be supported with a rear and/or front rest the targets used are more challenging. F-Class uses the same targets as NRA Target and International Target Rifle competitions, except that a specific F-Class target center is used at each yard line. The 10 ring of the 300-yard target is just 2.85 inches, and gets larger at greater distance with the 1,000-yard target center's 10 ring at 10 inches.

There are two divisions within the sport, Open and Target Rifle. In Open, the caliber limit is .35 and smaller, with the overall weight of the rifle not exceeding 10 kilograms (approximately 22 pounds). The Target Rifle Division features rifles limited to .223 or .308 caliber. Additional firearm modifications and equipment restrictions are listed in the rule book. The rifle weight must not exceed 8.25 kilograms (approximately 18.18 pounds). Competitors have just one minute per shot at the 300-, 500-, and 600-yard lines, and 1.5 minutes at the 800-, 900-, and 1,000-yard lines. There are a number of team and individual courses of fire that range from 40 shots to 180 shots and use either all target line distances or a combination of a portion of the distances. For a complete list of the courses of fire, look to the NRA F-Class rule book. Five ability classifications are recognized: High Master, Master, Expert, Sharpshooter, and Marksman.

NRA High-Power Sporting Rifle

NRA High-Power Sporting Rifle is a three-position event with shots fired from prone, sitting or kneeling, and standing. The rifles used are any centerfire rifles of any caliber that do not weigh more than 9.5 pounds. Additional firearm modifications and equipment restrictions are listed in the rule book. The two types of ammunition recognized are any safe ammunition and service ammunition, ammunition manufactured for and by the government issued for service use. Master, Expert, Sharpshooter, and Marksman are the four ability classes recognized in this sport.

The course features targets set at the 100- and 200-yard lines. The 100-yard has a 3.35-inch 10 ring, and the 200-yard target has a 7.0-inch 10 ring. Courses have a slow-fire portion where shooters have one minute to fire each shot, as well as a rapid-fire portion. In rapid fire, each shooter has just 30 seconds to fire four shots. There are a series of standard single-stage courses of fire that involve eight shots fired from the various positions at either the 100- or 200-yard targets. There are also standard multiple-stage or aggregate match courses of fire. The high-power sporting rifle match course consists of 32 shots: eight from prone, slow fire 100 or 200 yards, standing eight shots from slow fire 100 or 200 yards, sitting or kneeling, eight shots rapid fire from 100 or 200 yards, and prone eight shots rapid fire from 100 or 200 yards.

NRA High-Power Rifle

If you've seen pictures of the NRA National Matches at Camp Perry, Ohio, you know that NRA High-Power is a huge event. Not only do civilians compete, but branches of the military also send talented shooters to claim individual, team, and military service titles every year. Shots are fired from prone, kneeling, sitting, and standing at several target distances: 100, 200, 300, 500, 600, and 800-, 900-, and 1,000-yard targets. There are several divisions that include both metallic sights and optics, and they are Service Rifle, Any Rifle, NRA Match Rifle, NRA Any Sight Match Rifle/Tactical Rifle, and U.S. Palma Rifle.

The NRA's rule book on High-Power Rifle includes three full pages of different courses of fire, both single-stage and multiple-stage match courses using both slow- and rapid-fire portions at the different distances. In slow fire, for targets 500 yards and in, the time limit per shot is one minute. It's 1.5 minutes for 600 yards and beyond. Instead of a time limit per shot, some courses give a total overall time within which all shots must be completed for score. In the rapid-fire portion of the course of fire, shooters have 60 seconds to shoot 10 shots in the sitting or kneeling positions, and 70 seconds for 10 shots in prone. Five ability classifications are recognized: High Master, Master, Expert, Sharpshooter, and Marksman.

Service Rifle

Issued by the U.S. Armed Forces or of the same type and caliber, commercially manufactured rifles used in the Service Rifle division cannot have a trigger less than 4½ pounds. Standard stocks and slings must be used and external alterations are not allowed. Sights must be standard as issued. Specific rifle models allowed in service calibers are the M1, M14, M16, and M110.

Service Rifle Optic Sight

Service Rifle Optic Sight uses the same firearms listed above in the Service Rifle Division, but instead of metallic sights, there is no restriction and this division features top competitors using optics.

NRA Match Rifle

An NRA Match Rifle is a centerfire rifle with metallic sights that must be able to hold at least five rounds. Service rifles are considered match rifles unless otherwise specified in the rules.

NRA Any Sight Match Rifle/Tactical Rifle

This division uses any legal NRA Match Rifle with the added benefit of using any sight, so optics dominate the field. Bipods may be attached but not used in competition, and ammunition is restricted to .35 caliber or smaller.

U.S. Palma Rifle

Palma is a metallic-sight division only, and Palma rifles can be any rifle or service rifle chambered in .308 or .223 caliber NATO.

NRA Silhouette

Silhouette matches are essentially precision events using steel targets. Each steel plate must fall in order to score a hit. Where the shot impacts the steel can definitely affect whether or not the plate falls. Competitors have just one shot to knock down each steel target, and the course is fired in a five-shot series. To add to the fun and challenge, the shape of each target varies. Silhouettes of chickens are used at the closest distance, followed by strings of pigs, turkeys, and rams. Target size varies for pistol and rifle events based on the specific course of fire. Silhouette events differ from other NRA competitions in the classification system used as well. Instead of using the Master, Expert, Sharpshooter, and Marksman classes, this sport uses Master, AAA, AA, A, and B classes. There are both rifle and pistol sanctioned competitions. The main differences lie in the firearms used and the distances for each string of fire.

In Silhouette Pistol events, courses specify whether all shots must be fired from the standing position, with either one or both hands, or the freestyle position, where the shooter can fire from any safe position as long as the firearm is supported by only the body and not by any artificial or stabilizing means. Competitors have two minutes to fire at banks of five targets at each distance.

Hunter's Pistol Overview

This division is limited to pistols weighing less than 5 pounds and with an overall barrel length of less than 12 inches chambered in a range of calibers from .22 to .45. Bolt-action pistols are prohibited, and allowable external modifications are specified in the rule book. The course of fire consists of 40, 60, 80, or 120 shots fired in the standing position at targets at 40, 50, 75, and 100 meters or yards.

Hunter's Pistol (Any Sight)

Pistols that meet the requirements listed above that allow the use of optic sights.

Small-bore Hunter's Pistol (Any Sight)

This division is for pistols that meet the rule requirements of Hunter's Pistol but limited to .22 caliber only. Optics are allowed.

Hunter's Pistol Metallic Sights

This division is open to pistols that meet the requirements listed above, but only metallic sights are permitted.

Small-bore Hunter's Pistol Metallic Sights

This division is for pistols that meet the rule requirements of Hunter's Pistol, but is limited to .22 caliber only, and only metallic sights are permitted.

Long-Range Pistol Overview

Long-range pistols legal for silhouette competitions are described as either unlimited or conventional, with specifications listed below. The course of fire consists of 40, 60, 80, or 120 shots fired in the standing or freestyle position as specified in the course, at targets at 50, 100, 150, and 200 meters or yards for all but the Small-bore Divisions. For Small-bore the course is limited to either the standing or freestyle position, and targets are set at 40, 50, 75, and 100 meters or yards.

Unlimited Standing Long Range Pistol

The maximum weight of the handguns used in Unlimited Standing can be up to 8 pounds. Optic and telescopic sights are allowed in this division, but pistols are restricted to 15 inches in overall sight radius and barrel length.

Unlimited Small-bore Standing

This division is for pistols that meet the rule requirements of Unlimited Standing Long Range Pistol but are limited to .22 caliber only.

Unlimited Pistol

The rules for Unlimited Pistol are the same as for Unlimited Standing as listed above. However, in this division only metallic sights are permitted.

Unlimited Small-bore Pistol

This division is for pistols that meet the rule requirements of Unlimited Pistol but are limited to .22 caliber only.

Conventional Long-Range Pistol

This division features stock firearms that have been cataloged and are readily available to the public from firearms manufacturers. Only metallic sights are permitted, and the overall weight cannot exceed 5 pounds. Barrel length is limited to 12 inches, and only the specific external modification listed in the rules are allowed.

Conventional Small-bore Pistol

This division is for pistols that meet the rule requirements of Conventional Long Range Pistol but are limited to .22 caliber only.

Conventional Revolver

Firearms in this division must meet the requirements listed above of Conventional Long-Range Pistol but must be revolvers and can only be loaded with five rounds at a time.

Conventional Small-bore Revolver

This division is for pistols that meet the rule requirements of Conventional Long Range Pistol & Revolver but are limited to .22 caliber only.

Air Pistol Overview

There is also Pistol Silhouette for air pistols. The caliber cannot exceed .22, and there are two subcategories. Air Pistol is the unlimited division where optical sights are allowed. Air Pistol Open Sights restricts sights to approved metallic or open sights. The course of fire consists of 40, 60, 80, or 120 shots fired in the standing or freestyle position at targets at 10, 12.5, 15, and 18 yards.

As in Silhouette Pistol, in Silhouette Rifle events competitors have 2.5 minutes to fire at banks of five targets at each distance. Black Powder and Cowboy Lever Action Divisions have more liberal time requirements, which are specified below. All shots must be fired from the standing position without artificial support in all but Black Powder Cartridge events, where shooters fire from the standing position at the chicken silhouettes. At all other targets, the sitting or kneeling position is allowed with specific artificial support using cross-sticks. The rifle stock lies in the "V" made by crossing two appropriate sticks, and these are specifically permitted at the farther target distances for Black Powder events.

High Power Overview

This division is limited to rifles in 6mm caliber or larger. Stock and trigger modifications are specified in the NRA rule book. The course of fire consists of 40, 60, 80, or 120 shots fired in the standing position at targets at 200, 300, 385, and 500 meters or yards for all but the Small-bore divisions. The distances for Small-bore are 40, 60, 77, and 100 meters or yards.

High-Power Silhouette

Rifles in this division have a maximum barrel length of 30 inches. The weight limit is 10 pounds, 2 ounces, but there is an exception specifically for U.S. Rifle Models .30 M1, M1A, and M14. Any sights, metallic or telescopic, are allowed.

Small-bore Silhouette

This division is for rifles that meet the rule requirements of High-Power Silhouette but limited to .22 caliber only.

High Power Hunting Silhouette

Rifles with hunting-style stocks and barrels are permitted in this division. The maximum weight is 9 pounds, and there is a minimum trigger weight of 2 pounds. Any sights, metallic or telescopic, are allowed. Magazines must be loaded with a total of only five rounds.

Small-bore Hunting Silhouette

This division is for rifles that meet the rule requirements of High-Power Hunting Silhouette but are limited to .22 caliber only. Only single-loading rifles are permitted, and the weight of the rifle cannot exceed 8.5 pounds.

High-Power Semiautomatic Military Rifle

A division specifically for service rifles used by the U.S. Armed Forces with metallic sights. There is a 4.5-pound trigger weight minimum, and no external modifications are allowed.

Blackpowder Cartridge Rifle Overview

Hunting or military-style rifles with exposed hammers designed for blackpowder cartridges are permitted in these divisions. Only traditional blackpowder-style ammunition is allowed, with cast or lead bullets reminiscent of the type manufactured before 1896. The course of fire consists of 40, 60, 80, or 120 shots fired in the standing position at targets at 200, 300, 385 and 500 meters or yards. Slings are not allowed, but competitors have the option to use the support of cross-sticks at the 300-, 385-, and 500-meter positions.

Blackpowder Cartridge Rifle

Only metallic sights typical of the era are permitted in the Blackpowder Cartridge Rifle Division, and the maximum weight of the rifle is 12 pounds, 2 ounces.

Scoped Blackpowder Cartridge Rifle

The Scoped Blackpowder Division restricts rifles to 15 pounds maximum weight. Scopes are permitted, but the scope mount must be of the traditional style used in the blackpowder era.

Cowboy Lever Action Silhouette Overview

Designed as a grassroots competition for common hunting rifles, this division has three classes of Cowboy Lever Action Silhouette. Only metallic sights are allowed. Time limits are also more generous for this division. Competitors have two minutes to fire one shot on each target on a bank of five targets. The course of fire consists of 40, 60, 80, or 120 shots fired in the standing position, but target distance varies with each class as listed below.

Cowboy Lever-Action Silhouette

This class features lever-action, centerfire rifles with tubular magazines in .25 caliber or larger. Flat or roundnose rimmed case ammunition is required, with specified exceptions listed in the rule book. Target distances are 50, 100, 150, and 200 meters or yards.

Pistol Cartridge Cowboy Lever-Action Silhouette

Lever-action rifles with tubular magazines using rimmed pistol ammunition with round- or flat-nose bullets in pistol calibers are allowed in this class. Targets are set at 40, 50, 75, and 100 meters or yards.

Small-bore Cowboy Lever Action Silhouette

This is the .22 caliber class in Cowboy Silhouette, and any lever-action, pump, or semiautomatic rifle in .22 long rifle with a tubular magazine is permitted. Targets are set at 40, 50, 75, and 100 meters or yards.

Silhouette Air Rifle Overview

The Silhouette Air Rifle division features three classes of rifles that are Target Air Rifles, Sporter Air Rifles, or Open Air Rifles. Target Rifles must be unaltered factory, metallic-sight target rifles designed for competition. Sporter Air Rifles must be unaltered, readily available, cataloged rifles that weigh less than 11 pounds. Optics are allowed. Open Air Rifles have a 16-pound weight limit and a maximum barrel length of 40 inches. Optics are allowed. The course of fire consists of 40, 60, 80, or 120 shots fired in the standing or freestyle position at targets at 20, 30, 36, and 45 yards. Indoor courses are also allowed in air rifle with NRA approval.

NRA Precision Events

Sport Type: Precision

Scoring: Point

Targets: Paper or Steel Silhouette

Competition Scope: Local, state, and regional events with premier national championships.

Website: www.nrahq.org/compete

Guns & Gear:

- ✓ Single Firearm Sport
- ✓ Multi-Gun Sport (Some)
- ✓ Additional Specialized Gear Required

Competition Results & Standings:

- ✓ Competitors are classified by ability level
- ✓ Competitors are classified by firearm modifications
- ✓ Special Categories are recognized

Chapter 6 »

OLYMPIC SHOOTING SPORTS

Are you someone who is glued to the television every two years to watch the world's best athletes perform? Does the thought of winning an Olympic medal send chills up and down your spine? If the Olympics inspire you, then you might just want to try your hand at an Olympic shooting sport. Except for biathlon, most shooting sports in the Olympics are considered less physically intense than other sports. The challenge, though, lies in the ability to shoot extremely accurate shots, requiring precise coordination and an incredible mental game.

The International Shooting Sports Federation (ISSF) governs Olympic Shooting. There are currently fifteen shooting events in the Summer and Winter Olympic Games. Men and women compete separately, and all competitions use air guns, rimfire firearms, or shotguns. The Summer Games feature two types of competition, precision and clay target shooting. The Winter Games incorporate knockdown targets with cross-country skiing.

Did you know that one of the most accomplished Olympians happens to be a shooter? Kim Rhode has won numerous medals, including gold, in multiple Olympics. At the time of writing, Kim is preparing to be the first American athlete in history to win five medals in an individual sport in five consecutive Olympic Games. Photo courtesy of Kim Rhode and USA Shooting.

Rifle & Pistol

All rifle and pistol events in the Summer Olympics are precision-based and test the shooter's ability to hit a bull's-eye target with scoring rings. The rifles used in the competitions are incredibly accurate and are custom fit specifically to the shooter. Pistols meet specific criteria regarding weight, trigger pull, and grips. Air rifles and pistols shoot .177 caliber lead pellets. In Rimfire, .22 caliber firearms are used. Men and women both can strive for an Olympic medal in two air gun events and one 25-meter rimfire event each. The remaining events are all 50-meter rimfire events, with only one of these open to women.

Equipment Control is the organizing committee that provides gauges and instruments to ensure a shooter's equipment is legal for competition. All equipment must be registered and evaluated before each event. Grips, barrel dimensions, sights, electronic triggers, slings, jackets, trousers, gloves, and other gear are specifically measured for compliance with the rules. Shooters are issued an equipment control card that lists make, serial number, and caliber of each firearm used, and all approved equipment is marked with a seal. Once approved, this gear cannot be altered without having it reevaluated by Equipment Control. Shooters must keep their equipment control cards with them and bring them to the firing line when it's their turn to compete.

> **TIP:** Did you know that shooters can wear specific shooting clothing like shoes, gloves, trousers, and jackets in Olympic Rifle events? All clothing, even undergarments, is subject to the rules in these events.

Range officers ensure the safety of all participants on the range. Firearms must always be kept pointed downrange or within the target backstop area. Pit or technical officers manage all targets. All commands to move to the firing line, handle firearms, load, unload, and fire are given by range officials. Shooters are called to the line and given the opportunity to set up their equipment and handle firearms. Pre-competition Equipment Control verification checks are often completed at this time. The command "preparation time begins now" is issued, and the amount of time shooters have depends on the event. During preparation time the targets are visible and face the shooter. Shooters may dry fire or practice holding and aiming during this time.

The Chief Range Officer then issues commands for a Sighting Series. This is a series of shots that doesn't count for score and is only before the beginning of each competition. Sighter shots give shooters the opportunity to make sure their sights are dialed in and allow them to make any necessary sight adjustments before being given the command to "Start." Once the chief range officer issues the start command, every shot fired at this point is counted for score, and no more sighters are allowed. The competition stops at the command "Stop."

LINGO: *Shooters are allowed to use rifle rests, shooting mats, and kneeling rolls in Olympic Rifle events. All gear is subject to Equipment Control and must meet specific guidelines.*

In these precision sports, target systems have evolved from using one paper target per shot fired to electronic scoring systems that instantly provide feedback for each shot. The highest scoring ring on the target is a ten. These events feature two phases, a qualification and final. Qualification is open to all eligible competitors, and raw scores are tallied. Competitors have a time limit to complete a specified number of shots. Tie-breaker procedures are in place based on the highest number of tens, nines, eights, etc., and after that a shoot-off procedure is in place to establish ranking.

TIP: *Turning paper targets for Rapid Fire events have been replaced with electronic targets using a light system. Red light means don't shoot. Green means fire.*

Penalties are assessed for early and late shots, and if too many shots are fired. There are also specific rules that deal with shooters who have equipment malfunctions. Malfunctions are classified as either allowable or non-allowable. Procedures are in place for reshooting a series in the event a competitor has an allowable malfunction.

> **TIP:** *Did you know that all pistol shooting at the Olympics is one-handed, without any support? Wearing long sleeves? A range officer will physically check a shooter's wrist to make sure there is no hidden support.*

The final is reserved for the top eight competitors in all events except the 25m Men's Rapid Fire event, which takes only the top six. In the final, decimal point scores are used, measuring each shot closest to the center of the target to the tenth of a point. The highest score on an Olympic target is 10.9 and represents the centermost hit inside the 10 ring.

> **LINGO:** *Hits scored 10.6 or higher are often referred to as "deep" or "inner" tens.*

The final is arguably the most exciting aspect of competition in these precision sports. In the rifle and pistol events, commands are given for shooters to load and fire each shot within a specified time limit. After the time expires, scores are announced for each shooter until all ten shots in the final are fired and scored. It can be a nail-biter, and crowd interaction after each shot adds even more pressure. The competitor with the highest combined score from both phases wins the coveted Olympic Gold!

Men's & Women's 10m Air Rifle

In the air rifle events, competitors fire all shots from the standing position at a bull's-eye target positioned 10 meters from the firing line. The 10 ring is tiny, about the size of the very tip of a pencil at 0.5mm. Competitors are permitted to wear specialized shooting jackets, pants, and footwear. In the men's course, shooters fire 60 shots within one hour and 45 minutes. For the women's course, it's 40 shots within one hour and 15 minutes. A perfect score for men is 600, for women 400. The top eight battle for medal positions in the event final, where shooters have 75 seconds to fire one shot in each shot series.

Men's & Women's 10m Air Pistol

Like the air rifle event, air pistol tests ultimate accuracy. Competitors fire all shots one-handed, unsupported from the standing position at a bull's-eye target positioned 10 meters from the firing line. In this event, the 10 ring is smaller than half an inch. Like air rifle, in the men's course, competitors fire 60 shots within one hours and 45 minutes. For the women's course, it's 40 shots within one hour and 15 minutes. A perfect score for men is 600, for women 400. The top eight battle for medal positions in the event final, where shooters have 75 seconds to fire one shot in each shot series.

Men's 25-Meter Rapid Fire

Men's Rapid Fire is the speed event of the Olympic shooting sports. Competitors fire all shots one-handed, unsupported from the standing position at five bull's-eye targets positioned 25 meters from the firing line. Events once used turning paper targets, but now feature a light system.

The course is 60 shots divided into two stages. Each stage is divided into six, five-shot series. In each series one shot is fired at each of five targets with a 10 ring that is about 4 inches wide. Before the beginning of the stage, the shooter may fire one sighter series of five shots in 8 seconds. After the sighters there are two, 8-second series, followed by two, 6-second shot series, and finally two, 4-second series.

> **TIP:** *The main difference between .22 long rifle and .22 short is the length of the case and the amount of powder charge used. Because the case is shorter, there is less capacity for gunpowder. .22 caliber short shoots "softer" and when it was allowed in Olympic Rapid Fire, it was desirable for faster shot-to-shot recovery. Competitors in Rapid Fire now use .22 long rifle.*

Unique to Men's Rapid Fire and Women's 25m Sport Pistol, shooters must assume a "ready" position. The ready is the start position before each series, where the shooter's firing arm is pointed downward at an angle of not greater than 45 degrees from the vertical. The arm cannot be pointed directly at the ground within the forward edge of the firing point. The arm has to remain stationary in this position until the green light indicating the command to fire comes on. Raising the arm too soon or not lowering it sufficiently will result in warnings and possible penalties.

The range officer gives specific commands for each series, before issuing the command to load. When given the command to load, shooters have one minute to load only five rounds into their pistols. After one minute has expired, the command "attention" is given, and red lights turn on. Next comes the command "3-2-1-START," and once the green light comes on, pistols can be raised and shooters fire shots within the time limits for the specific series. Red lights indicate the time to stop shooting, and any shots fired during this period do not count for score.

Only the top six shooters compete in the event final. Shooters who make the final fire four, five-shot series in the 4-second time limit. Decimal point scoring is used to determine the winner.

Women's 25-Meter Pistol

This event is also known as Women's Sport Pistol. Like Men's Rapid Fire, competitors fire all shots one-handed, unsupported from the standing position. Only .22 long rifle caliber pistols are used to shoot at bull's-eye targets positioned 25 meters from the firing line. Electronic targets with the red/green light system are now predominantly used for this course.

There are two stages in the event. The first is a precision stage shot in six, five-shot series for a total of 30 shots. Shooters have five minutes to complete each series of five shots. The target used for this portion of the match has a 10 ring that's close to the size of a golf ball.

The second stage is the rapid-fire portion. The 10 ring for the rapid-fire target is close to 4 inches wide. This portion is fired in 5-shot series all on a single target for a total of 30 shots. After the command to load, shooters have one minute to load their pistols with five rounds only and assume the ready position as described in the Men's Rapid Fire section above. The command "attention" is issued, and the red lights are switched on. When the target lights turn green, the competitor has 3 seconds to raise the pistol and take the shot before the green light switches back to red. The 3-second shot time is followed by 7 seconds of rest in the ready position. The competitor cannot rest the firearm on the bench or shooting table at any time during the series. After a delay of 7 seconds the green light will come on once again. The same procedure is repeated until all five shots of the string have been fired.

The top eight shooters compete in the event final. Shooters who make the final fire four of the five-shot rapid-fire series. Decimal point scoring is used to determine the winner.

Men's 50-Meter Rifle Prone

The 50-Meter Rifle Prone is a men's-only event. Competitors fire all shots from the prone position, lying on their stomachs, at a bull's-eye target positioned 50 meters from the firing line with .22 caliber rifles. The 10 ring is smaller than a dime at a mere 10.4 mm in diameter. Competitors fire all 60 shots from the prone position within one hour and 15 minutes for a possible perfect score of 600 points. The top eight battle for medal positions in the 10-shot event final, where shooters have 45 seconds to complete each shot.

Men's 50-Meter Pistol

Another event just for men, 50-Meter Pistol is often referred to as Free Pistol. Competitors fire all shots with .22 caliber pistols one-handed, unsupported from the standing position at a bull's-eye target positioned 50 meters from the firing line. In this event the 10 ring is about 2 inches wide. In the qualification portion of the match, competitors have an unlimited number of sighters and have two hours to fire 60 shots for score. A perfect score in this phase is 600. The finals feature decimal scoring, and the top eight competitors have 75 seconds to shoot 10 shots.

Men's & Women's 50-Meter Three-Position Rifle

Three-Position Rifle features shots from standing, kneeling, and prone positions at a bull's-eye target positioned 50 meters from the firing line. As with the 50m Prone event, the 10 ring is 10.4mm in diameter. Shots must be fired in prone first, followed by standing, and the kneeling position is last. In the men's course, competitors fire a total of 120 shots divided into 40-shot increments. In events using electronic targets, shooters have 45 minutes to fire 40 shots from prone, one hour and 15 minutes for 40 shots standing, and one hour to shoot 40 shots in the kneeling position. A perfect score is 1200. In the women's qualification match, competitors fire a total of 60 shots, 20 from each position. Women have an overall maximum time of two hours and 15 minutes. The perfect score for women is 600. The top eight battle for medal positions in the 10-shot event final using decimal scoring. Shooters have 75 seconds to fire each shot from the standing position, for a total of 10 shots.

SCORECARD

USA Shooting Precision Rifle & Pistol

Sport Type: Precision

Scoring: Points

Targets: Paper or Electronic

Competition Scope: Local, state, and regional events with premier national, continental, world championships and Olympic Events

Website: www.usashooting.org

Guns & Gear:
- ✓ Single Firearm Sport
- ☐ Multi-Gun Sport
- ✓ Additional Specialized Gear Required

Competition Results & Standings:
- ✓ Competitors are classified by ability level
- ☐ Competitors are classified by firearm modifications
- ✓ Special Categories are recognized

Shotgun Sports

Trap, double trap, and skeet are the three Olympic Shotgun events. Competitors shoot from stations at orange clay disks thrown from traps. Referees maintain safety and order, and direct competitors throughout the match. They also score the targets. In order for a target to count as a hit, a referee must confirm that at least one visible piece of the target has been broken by the shot. Targets that are missed or "dusted," where no visible piece is broken, become "lost" targets.

> **LINGO:** *"No bird" is a command issued by the referee when a target is not thrown properly, is already broken, is irregular in color, or some sort of error occurs with the target launch.*

Competitors may use either conventional double-barreled or semiautomatic smoothbore shotguns, in 12-gauge or smaller. The addition of compensators and similar devices fitted to the barrel is allowed in skeet, but not in any of the trap events. Ported barrels and ported interchangeable chokes are permitted, but are subject to specific parameters. Optical sights or any device that magnifies or visually enhances the target are specifically prohibited.

Each trap machine is set and tuned precisely for each competition to a specific angle, height, and distance. The ranges are set, examined, and approved by a jury to make sure the competition is fair and consistent.

Shooting occurs only under the supervision of the referee. Shots may be fired only when it is the shooter's turn and the target has been thrown. Because shooters move from station to station, firearms must be carried empty, with the breech visibly open and the muzzle pointed in a safe direction at all times. Shotguns not in use must be secured in a safe, case, or stand. All shotguns must be kept unloaded except on the shooting station, and then only after the command to start has been given. Shooters may turn or exit the shooting station only once their shotgun is open and empty. In preparation to shoot, aiming is permitted only at specific stations and with the permission of the referee.

Qualification rounds establish who will have a chance to compete in the event final. The six shooters with the best results compete in this round to decide the overall winner. The final in trap and skeet events is 25 targets. For Men's Double Trap, the final consists of 50 targets.

> **TIP:** *Shoot the same score? No worries, there is an established shoot-off procedure to determine tie-breakers for shotgun events.*

What else do you need to know? Take a look at the ISSF rule book for clothing rules. Wearing camouflage, too-short shorts, or sleeveless T-shirts is specifically not allowed.

Trap & Doubles Trap

In a sequence of trap, shooters are assigned in squads to shoot 25 targets through a series of five adjacent shooting stations. Each squad member is assigned a shooting order and must arrive at the station with sufficient ammunition and all equipment necessary to complete the round. The referee gives all start commands. When the first shooter is ready, he or she raises the gun to the shoulder and calls out "pull," "go," or some other appropriate command. Upon the command, the target immediately launches from an underground bunker and flies downrange, moving away from the shooter. Two shots may be fired at each target before it disappears, except in the finals and in Doubles Trap, where competitors can fire only one shot at each target.

In Men's Trap, competitors shoot five rounds of 25 targets for a total of 125 qualification targets and 25 targets for the six shooters who make the final. For Women's Trap, it's three rounds of 25, totaling 75 targets, and 25 targets in the final. Men's Double Trap is 150 total targets shot in three rounds of 50 each, and the finals consists of 50 targets. Trap events can take place over two or three days and can be shot in a number of different sequences.

Skeet

As with trap shooting, competitors fire at birds from stations. Unlike trap, where the shooter begins with shotgun shouldered, skeet shooters must assume a ready position before giving the "pull" command. In the ready position, the shooter must stand with both feet entirely within the shooting station boundaries. The gun must be held with both hands, and the gunstock must be in contact with shooter's body. The entire stock of the shotgun must be below the official ISSF marker tape and be clearly visible to the referee. Not just any old piece of tape, the marker tape is set when all pockets of the shooting vest are empty. With the trigger arm touching the body, the shooter's elbow must then be bent into a fully closed upward angle position, with no awkward list of the shoulders.

In skeet, there are also specific target shooting sequences for all qualification and final rounds. Targets are launched as either singles (one bird) or doubles (two birds). Skeet also differs from trap in that targets fly across the range in front of the shooter—in trap, targets are launched away from the shooter. There are eight stations set up in a semicircle, and at each station a specific target order is issued. This order can be a combination of either single or double targets coming out high or low from the traps on either side of the range. Because this course is always the same, shooters know that they can load only one cartridge when firing at a single. Two cartridges are allowed for firing at doubles. If a shooter only loads one round for a double, the second target is deemed "lost."

In men's skeet, competitors shoot five rounds of 25 targets, for a total of 125 targets. The six top scoring shooters then compete in a 25-target final. For women's skeet, competitors shoot three rounds of 25 targets for a total of 75 targets before establishing the top six shooters for the final.

SCORECARD

USA Shooting Shotgun

Sport Type: Shotgun

Scoring: Hit/Miss

Targets: Clay Disks

Competition Scope: Local, state, and regional events with premier national, continental, world championships and Olympic Events

Website: www.usashooting.org

Guns & Gear:
- ✓ Single Firearm Sport
- ☐ Multi-Gun Sport
- ✓ Additional Specialized Gear Required

Competition Results & Standings:
- ✓ Competitors are classified by ability level
- ☐ Competitors are classified by firearm modifications
- ☐ Special Categories are recognized

Biathlon

The only shooting sport in the Winter Olympic Games, biathlon combines the endurance of cross-country skiing with rifle shooting from the standing and prone positions. It's a delicate balance of racing against the clock, yet taking the time to hit all targets because misses result in penalties. Shooters fire at five steel targets set in banks at 50 meters from the firing line. From the prone position, targets are smaller than 2 inches. In the standing position they are about 4.5 inches. Once hit, black targets flip to expose white, making for a sport that's very spectator-friendly.

Men and women compete in five different biathlon events in the Winter Olympics: individual, relay, spring, pursuit, and mass start. Shooters carry their rifles with them from point to point, slung across their backs. Bolt-action .22 caliber rifles without optics are used for biathlon events, and competitors can only load a specific number of rounds for each event.

Men's & Women's Individual

In the men's and women's individual event, shooters ski around 3- to 4-kilometer loops, a total of five times. After each loop, the shooter must complete four firing stages of five rounds in the following sequence: prone, standing, prone, standing. For each miss, one minute is added to the shooter's total time. Start of the individual match is at intervals, with a shooter starting every 30 seconds. Shooters may only load and shoot five rounds, one for each target. In the men's individual event, athletes race for a total of 20 kilometers. The women's individual event is a 15-kilometer race.

Men's & Women's Sprint

As in the individual event, competitors in the sprint competition are started at 30-second intervals. Athletes start out on skis for a total distance of between 3 and 4 kilometers. Next, the athletes fire from the prone position, followed by the second portion of skiing. Firing from the standing position is last. Unlike the individual event, where time is added directly to an athlete's score for misses, in the Sprint, competitors must ski a 150-meter handicap loop for every miss. The more a shooter misses, the more he or she has to ski. Shooters may only load and shoot five rounds, one for each target. The men's sprint is a total of 10 kilometers. The women's sprint is 7.5 kilometers.

Men's & Women's Relay

Competition is fierce and exciting in the relay, a team event with a simultaneous start by the first member of each team. Teams of four athletes must each ski the course, stopping twice to shoot, first from prone and then from the standing position. Shooters tag the next teammates in a handover zone. Unlike other biathlon events, in relay shooters can load up to eight rounds to shoot their five targets, but they can only load five to start. If a shooter misses, he or she must handload each single round until the target is hit. The men's relay consists of four shooters, each racing 7.5 kilometers. The women's relay is four shooters each skiing 6 kilometers.

Men's & Women's Pursuit

The pursuit is an event based on finish times in previous competition and is limited to only 60 athletes. The order in which they start the course is based on their overall finish. Unlike other events, where shooters may choose their firing line, athletes must line up at firing positions based on the order they enter the range, making this a very dynamic competition. The shooting sequence is prone, prone, standing, and standing. As with the sprint event, misses result in a trip to the 150-meter penalty loop. Because the competition is based on standings, especially with how shooters line up on the range, it is appropriately named the pursuit event. The total distance skied in men's pursuit is 12.5 kilometers. For women the distance is 10 kilometers.

Men's & Women's Mass Start

As the name indicates, mass start means a simultaneous start for all competitors but is open to only the top 30 athletes. With all the athletes on line, starting at the same time, this event can be a nail-biter. As in the pursuits, the firing sequence is prone, prone, standing, standing, with men skiing a total distance of 15 kilometers. Women ski 12.5 kilometers. As in the original biathlon events (except for the individual events), shooters who miss a target must ski a 150-meter penalty loop.

> **TIP:** *How can you enjoy biathlon in summer months? Compete in Summer Biathlon! Instead of skiing and shooting, competitors run and shoot.*

SCORECARD

Team USA Biathlon

Sport Type: Precision

Scoring: Hit/Miss

Targets: Steel

Competition Scope: Local, state, and regional events with premier national, continental, world championships and Olympic Events

Website: www.biathlon.teamusa.org

Guns & Gear:
- ✓ Single Firearm Sport
- ☐ Multi-Gun Sport
- ✓ Additional Specialized Gear Required

Competition Results & Standings:
- ☐ Competitors are classified by ability level
- ☐ Competitors are classified by firearm modifications
- ✓ Special Categories are recognized

Chapter 7 »

SHOTGUN SPORTS

Are you the type of person who likes instant gratification? Looking for a shooting sport with minimal investment and that's easy to get into? Shotgun sports are very popular shooting sports because many people own shotguns already. For those who don't own them, shotguns can often be easily purchased compared to other firearms. Ammunition is readily available and relatively inexpensive. Shotgun sports also provide exciting, instant feedback when a clay bursts into a puff of orange dust. Many who compete in shotgun sports find them addictive.

There are three main types of shotgun sports in the United States. They are skeet, trap, and sporting clays. In skeet, targets fly across the range from right to left and left to right in front of the shooter. In trap, shooters fire at clay targets that are launched so that they fly away from the shooter. Sporting clays is the most dynamic of the shotgun sports, and competitors fire at a wide variety of targets that fly or "run" across the range and move through the air both toward and away from the shooter.

Scoring is universal for all three sports and targets are referred to as "dead" or "lost." A dead target is one where a visible piece is broken before the targets strikes the ground. Lost is the term used

With so many clay target ranges in the United States, shotgun sports offer one of easiest ways to get started in shooting competitions.

for targets that have not been broken after the shot has been fired. Referees determine whether targets are scored as dead. Procedures are in place for target malfunctions and irregular targets thrown. Even though a referee or range officer is present, the shooter is responsible for loading the correct number of shells and the correct type of shell for each position. There are rules that accommodate gun malfunctions and failed ammunition. Scores are based on the total number of dead targets in a round.

Skeet

The National Skeet Shooting Association (NSSA) governs skeet shooting in the United States. Targets are clay discs that measure no more than $4\frac{5}{16}$ inches in diameter and $1\frac{1}{8}$ inches in height. Clays are launched from houses located on the right and left sides of the range. In skeet, targets are launched across the range, either as single targets or double targets depending on the event.

Shotguns used must be capable of firing two shots. Double-barreled shotguns, both side-by-sides and over-and-unders, as well as semi-autos and pump guns can be used. There are several divisions in skeet, based on the shotgun gauge the competitor is using. These include 12-, 20-, and 28-gauge, and .410 bore. (Note that for .410 shotguns, the number designates a caliber—as in rifles and handguns—rather than a gauge, as is used for other shotgun sizes.) Allowable shot load sizes are specified for each division, but no shot smaller than No. 9 shot (2mm) or larger than 7½ may be used.

Special categories are recognized and are referred to as concurrent events in the sport, for various ages of veterans, seniors, and juniors, as well as ladies, military, and retired military. Two- or five-person teams can also participate, and events often feature shoot-offs as well. Classification in skeet is measured using letters, with AAA being the highest, down to E class.

The skeet field uses eight shooting stations. Imagine a semi-circle with the flat base closest to downrange, and with the curve of the circle facing uprange. Station 1 is located at the left end of the circle, and stations 2 through 7 follow the curve of the circle. Station 8 is located in the middle, at the center of the base of the semicircle. Clay targets or birds fly from each of the houses on either side of the circle, one from the high house and one from the low house. There are shooting boundary limits marked at 44 yards and 60 yards. A target crossing point is designated, and each clay must pass within a specific distance of the crossing point and also travel a minimum distance from the skeet house in order to ensure consistency throughout the course.

All shots must be fired with both feet inside the boundaries of the shooting position. The shooter has the option to hold the shotgun in any safe position he or she finds comfortable. The shooter yells "Pull!" or some other start signal to indicate readiness to shoot, resulting in a target thrown within the next second.

A standard squad in skeet has five shooters. The squad shoots a "round" of skeet, 25 shots, with the object to break as many clays as possible. The squad starts at Station 1 with the first competitor shooting a pair of singles, calling "Pull!" for a target from the high house and then "Pull!" again for a clay from the low house. The shooter then shoots a double, calling "Pull!" only once and shooting a target from the nearest house first, then immediately followed by the clay thrown from the farthest house from the station.

The same procedure is followed by all shooters in the squad, and then repeated at Station 2. At Stations 3 through 5 only singles are fired. The first shooter fires at a single clay launched from the high house, followed by one from the low house. From Station 6, singles are fired first from the high house and then from the low house before shooting doubles. Unlike Station 1, for doubles at Station 6, the shooter fires at the low house target first and the high house target second. The same procedure is followed at Station 7. At Station 8, each shooter shoots one clay from the high house. Then all shooters shoot a target from the low house. If a competitor has no lost targets, he or she has the option to shoot the low house for the 25th shot of the round.

In addition to the traditional round of skeet, other events are held. Skeet can be fired in doubles, where a minimum of 50 clays are launched from the high and low houses. The NSSA also allows for a special event called Event 6, designed to encourage new shooters to shoot the guns they already own. Competitors may use any gun of any gauge, as long as ammunition meets NSSA's specifications. Everyone is welcome and eligible for awards.

Trap

The Amateur Trapshooting Association (ATA) governs trap shooting in the United States. Targets are clay disks that measure no more than $4^{5}/_{16}$ inches in diameter and $1^{1}/_{8}$ inches in height. Targets are launched from trap houses that are set at specific heights. Clays are set to fly away from the shooting position downrange at different angles specified in the rules. In trap, shooters can compete in singles and/or doubles events.

Shotguns capable of firing two shots in 12-gauge or smaller are used, including double-barreled shotguns, both side-by-side and over-and-under, as well as semiautos and pump shotguns. Several rules apply to ammunition, with some specifically disallowed in trap events. As in skeet and sporting clays, though, no shot size larger than $7^{1}/_{2}$ may be used.

Special categories are recognized for Lady, Sub-Junior, Junior, Veteran, and Senior Veteran competitors. As in skeet, events can feature shoot-offs as well. Shooters are grouped by ability into a letter-based classification, AAA, AA, A, B, C, and D classes.

There are two main events in amateur trap, both shot from 16 yards. They are called singles and doubles events. All shots are fired from posts, which designate the shooting positions, which are laid out in an arc 4 yards apart. In the singles event, 5 or 10 shots are fired from each of five shooting posts. In the doubles event, two clays are launched instead of one. All targets that are launched from the houses must be within a minimum and maximum distance and from specified heights. The ATA uses a handicap system for new shooters.

Sporting Clays

The National Sporting Clays Association (NSCA) governs sporting clays within the United States. Any regulation clay target can be used, and these are launched from traps to mimic the wild game typically taken with a shotgun. Where trap and skeet are fixed courses of fire where the shooter can expect to shoot an identical presentation of targets for every event, sporting clays events vary from match to match. Competitors may shoot targets that fly away from them, at them, from the sides of the range, along the ground, and straight up into the air. The NSCA allows event officials freedom to design courses with minimal restrictions. Shoot officials determine the number of stations, the numbers and types of targets launched from each station, and the number of fields for a given event.

Shotguns used must be capable of firing two shots, and there are several divisions based on the gauge the competitor is using. These include 12-, 20-, and 28-gauge and .410 bore. Allowable shot load sizes are specified for each division, but no shot smaller than No. 9 shot (2mm) or larger than 7½ may be used. Special categories are also recognized as concurrent events for veterans, junior competitors, and ladies. Shooters are classified based on ability in Master, AA, A, B, C, D, and E classes.

All shots are fired from shooting stations. A field is a group of stations. Shooters compete in all stations of a field before moving on to the next field. Shooters either fire in squads of three to six people, or in a format called a European Rotation. Squads shoot the entire course, field to field, in a fixed sequence. In European Rotation, a start time and end time are established. It becomes the responsibility of each competitor to ensure that they complete the entire event within the specified time frame.

The start position is either low gun or one where the shooter begins with the gun mounted to the shoulder. The shooter yells "Pull!" or some other start signal to indicate readiness to shoot, which results in one or two targets being thrown. Clays are either presented as single targets or as pairs, in which case two shots are allowed and the target is scored dead if broken by either shot or as a pair. With pairs, only two shots are allowed. Pairs are either classified as reports, following, or simultaneous. In a report pair, one bird is launched and after the first shot, the second bird is launched. In a following pair, the first clay target is thrown and is followed by the second clay within the time established by the designing official. A simultaneous pair is one where both birds are thrown at the same time. Targets are scored as hits, dead/lost, or missed.

Five-stand is a specific type of sporting clays event consisting of targets shot from five shooting stands with six to eight traps. Shooters rotate from station to station, and traps launch clays simulating gamebirds. The types of clays thrown include running rabbits along the ground and traps launching clays that simulate gamebirds flying through the air from various directions, both toward and away from the shooter.

SCORECARD

Shotgun Sports

Sport Type: Shotgun

Scoring: Hit/Miss

Targets: Clay Disks

Competition Scope: Local, state, and regional events with premier national and world championships.

Websites: NSSA & NSCA - www.nssa-nsca.org
ATA - www.shootata.com

Guns & Gear:
- ✓ **Single Firearm Sport**
- ☐ **Multi-Gun Sport**
- ☐ **Additional Specialized Gear Required**

Competition Results & Standings:
- ✓ **Competitors are classified by ability level**
- ☐ **Competitors are classified by firearm modifications**
- ✓ **Special Categories are recognized**

Chapter 8 »

HANDGUN ACTION SHOOTING SPORTS

Do you get bored doing the same thing over and over again? Are you looking for a shooting sport that has possible practical applications? Perhaps you are interested in a more physical shooting sport. Action shooting sports are fast and furious! They represent the most dynamic shooting sports on the circuit. These events require advanced gun handling and shooting skills that are frequently tested in the heat of competition. Just to name a few, competitors can expect to draw from the holster, speed reload, load the gun on the clock, fire with just one hand, shoot at both stationary and moving targets, and shoot on the move.

Back in 1976 in Columbia, Missouri, a group of individuals including Col. Jeff Cooper (1920–2006), considered the founding father of modern pistol techniques, met to talk about a shooting sport that evaluated skills with handguns that were commonly carried for personal defense. Law enforcement officers and law-abiding citizens wanted to create an official sport that helped them improve both shooting and gun handling in practical scenarios with the guns they

Just how good is Rob Leatham? In a winning career that has spanned over three decades, Rob has won national and world titles in every single action shooting sport listed in this chapter and is known as "TGO—The Great One" in action shooting.

carried every day. The International Practical Shooting Confederation (IPSC) was born.

It didn't take long for the sport to catch on, with events popping up all over the globe. The United States Practical Shooting Association (USPSA) was formed, governing practical competitions throughout the United States. With the excitement, offshoot organizations sprang up. John Bianchi founded the first Bianchi Cup Championships, (now called the NRA Bianchi Cup), an invitation-only event that offered big cash to the winner in 1979. Steel Challenge was born in 1981, an all-steel, pure speed course of fire with the first match held in Piru, California. Another all-steel event, the American Handgunner Shoot-Off, was an annual world championship where competitors mowed down steel targets in a man-vs.-man style shoot-off. In 1986 the first Masters International Championships were held in Barry, Illinois, and tested shooters' skills in both precision and speed events. The Sportsman Team Challenge combined action shooting with silhouette and sporting clays in a premier team event that was even sponsored by Chevrolet! Revolver shooters formed their own sport, the International Confederation of Revolver Enthusiasts (ICORE), and held the first International Revolver Championships in 1991. In two decades, the sport grew exponentially, both in participants and unique competitions.

From the 1980s to the 1990s the best shooters in the world donned the colors and logos of major manufacturers, and shooting events were even featured on the cable network ESPN. Today IPSC has shooters in more than 85 countries participating in the sport. Competitors from around the world come together once every three years to compete at the IPSC World Shoot, one of the grandest events in action shooting. USPSA has grown as well, and developed State, Sectional, and Area events. UPSPA is now an organization with nearly 20,000 members.

In the 1990s, when USPSA failed to develop divisions suitable for entry-level competitors, the International Defensive Pistol Association (IDPA) was formed. This back-to-the-roots form of shooting addressed the need for shooting divisions dedicated to factory stock firearms, and also featured courses of fire with a more defensive flair. IDPA has grown to over 15,000 members since forming in 1996.

Some events have thrived, others have died out, and still others are on their way to successful comebacks. American Handgunner is no more, though several clubs have tried to resurrect the most nail-biting, spectator-friendly event in the shooting sports. The Masters

Championship is still held at the same time, same place every year, but participation is low and the level of competition continues to dwindle. Sportsman Team Challenge no longer attracts significant numbers of big-name shooters and manufacturer-sponsored teams. The Bianchi Cup was once a sellout event that required an invitation, but because of low participation for a number of years, hard-to-come-by invitations became a thing of the past. Addressing some rule changes and working to spread the word about the event, Bianchi is on its way back to being one of the most prestigious events on the circuit. Steel Challenge took a hiatus for a number of years but made a successful comeback in the late 1990s. Once just a single match each year, Steel Challenge was acquired by USPSA in 2007 and has developed state, regional, and national championships.

Why the rise and fall? Action shooting sports have evolved from grassroots-level events where competitors could show up with the firearms they own to matches where highly specialized, expensive equipment is required to place high in the results. The sports that thrive today allow for both high-end custom guns and entry-level guns, the kind you can buy at your local gun shop. Single events with no developed program at the local, state, and regional levels find that the competition is stiff when vying for shooters as customers.

To an outsider, the coming and going of action shooting events might appear to be as dynamic as the courses of fire. Unlike the NRA, USA Shooting, or ISSF, there is no body that oversees all action shooting sports. Because action shooting events often use targets that are humanoid in shape and require advanced gun handling skills, these competitions are admittedly and proudly the most politically incorrect. They are also some of the easiest shooting sports to try. For that reason alone, they deserve a significant amount of attention in this book. Let's take a look at the major handgun action shooting sports.

International Practical Shooting Confederation (IPSC)

Accuracy, power, and speed are equivalent elements in IPSC, and the sport uses the acronym DVC in Latin as a tag line: *Diligentia, Vis, Celeritas* (Accuracy, Power, Speed). Matches are freestyle in nature, meaning that competitors are given every opportunity to solve the course-of-fire challenge as they see fit, shooting targets from where they are visible. Some courses may limit what shooters can do, or dictate how they must engage targets, but this happens only for specific stages or to prevent safety issues. Shooting boxes and fault lines provide physical and visual references for competitors and establish the boundaries of the acceptable shooting area for each stage. Obstacles, barriers, and other stage props are used in courses to further add to the excitement.

Due to the physical nature and advanced gun handling skills in practical shooting, there are extensive safety rules. In addition to following course-of-fire procedures, all competitors must adhere to strict safety rules that include keeping the fingers outside the trigger guard while loading, unloading, or reloading, as well as while moving, unless a competitor is safely engaging targets. Firearms can only be handled in designated safety areas or under the direct supervision and direction of a range officer. Unless otherwise specified, a competitor's muzzle cannot pass safety demarcations referred to as the 90-degree mark, measured from the front of the competitor facing directly downrange. At no time can competitors cross themselves or someone else with the muzzles of their firearms, an unsafe movement known as "sweeping." Unsafe shots fired where the bullet does not impact the berm, or impacts the ground closer than 10 feet from the competitor (unless engaging a safe target) are also disqualifying offenses. Unsafe gun handling of any kind, unsportsmanlike conduct, and the use of prohibited substances (drugs and alcohol) is not tolerated.

Guns are carried in holsters, and magazines and speed loaders in pouches on a shooter's belt. How the belt can be set up is specific to the division the competitor is shooting in. Shooters are not allowed to move their gear around once a competition begins, and the locations of the holster and magazine pouches on the belt are recorded on an equipment card for verification purposes. Competitors must wear all holsters and ammunition holders at waist level. To allow for the curves of the female body, women are permitted to wear their holsters at hip level so that the position from which they draw the gun is similar to that of their male competitors. Popular among practical shooters, companies offer an inner and outer belt system.

The belt (both inner and outer), holster, and magazine pouches are collectively referred to as a shooter's rig.

The inner belt is a Velcro belt that is threaded through belt loops. The outer belt attaches to the inner belt. This kind of system keeps the setup consistent on shooters' bodies each time they wear it.

In all divisions, the holster and ammunition holders cannot be more than 50mm (2 inches) from the competitor's inner belt. The heel of the butt of the handgun must be above the top of the belt. While holstered, the gun cannot point farther than 1 meter (3 feet in the U.S.) from the competitor's feet when standing relaxed. Additional holster restriction may apply to the different divisions.

IPSC matches feature both paper and steel targets. Only two paper targets are approved in IPSC matches, the classic target and a miniature version of the classic. These targets are shaped like an eight-sided shield with three scoring rings. No-shoot targets, as the name implies, are clearly marked penalty targets that serve as vision barriers, and also can be used to make shoot targets more difficult. The classic target is simply reversed to show a white side, indicating a no-shoot. A scored hit on a no-shoot target results in a penalty, reducing the shooter's point score. Targets can also be marked with soft or hard cover. Soft cover merely obscures targets, and shots that pass through soft cover score. Hard cover is deemed impenetrable, and any bullets that pass through hard cover cannot score on the target. An assortment of steel targets are approved for use in competition. Plates of varying sizes and shapes can be used, as well as targets called classic poppers. There are even miniature versions of these targets, and steel must fall to score unless otherwise specified in the course.

Chronographs are used to determine the power factor of every competitor's ammunition, and the minimum caliber used in matches is 9mm. Power factor is the velocity of the bullet used multiplied by the weight of the bullet, measured in grains. The premise behind power factor is that the founders of the sport wanted to award higher points to those who fired powerful ammunition. The idea that major power factor ammo had more knockdown power, as well as more

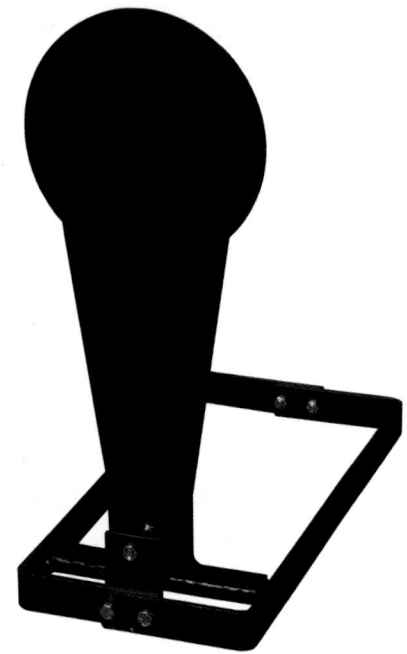

Both steel and paper targets are used in IPSC competition. The classic paper target has three scoring zones, and the classic popper steel target must fall to score.

recoil, and therefore should score more points, was in effect. Power factor has remained an important part of competition scoring in this sport to this day. The minimum power factor for IPSC for minor is consistent across the board for all divisions, at 125. For major scoring, the minimum power factor varies depending on the division.

Whether a competitor is scored major or minor determines the number of points they receive for hits on target. On the classic target, the A zone is worth the five maximum points for both major and minor. For the C zone, four points are awarded to major and three point to minor. Hits in the D zone are worth two points in major and just one point in minor.

Scoring can be a bit confusing, and the different divisions are scored separately. Standings are based on hit factors for each course of fire. A hit factor is the shooter's total accumulated points on targets, divided by the time it took to complete a stage. The highest hit factor on a given stage wins the stage and is awarded the most stage points allotted for that course of fire. Stage points are based on the number of targets and their maximum point value. A competitor's stage points are then added up for all stages in the match to give a total match point score. The shooter with the most match points is awarded 100 percent and the overall title. All other shooters are given a percentage of the winner's overall point total to determine the rest of the scores and rankings within in the match.

There are three types of courses of fire in IPSC. Comstock courses allow shooters to take as many shots as they like on a stipulated number of targets, with the number of hits specified for each target. Some courses designate a specific number of shots per target, and extra shots and extra hits are penalized. This type of scoring is called Virginia Count. The third type of scoring is Fixed Time, and a specific number of shots can be fired at specific targets within a specified time. Penalties are assessed for extra hits, extra shots, and late shots. Procedural penalties can also be assessed for shooting outside a fault line or shooting box, failing to perform a mandatory reload, or any other failure to follow the course-of-fire description properly in all types of courses.

Except in courses used for classification purposes, a competitor may never shoot the same course of fire twice in their shooting career. Depending on the size of an event, there can be as few as just a handful of stages in a match, to more than 30. Courses of fire are designated by size—small, medium, and large. A specific ratio is used at each major event in order to ensure that skills are tested. There are also five different levels of events that cover IPSC regions, continental championships, and up to the World Championships.

At the beginning of each course of fire, competitors are given a stage briefing. The briefing includes details about how the stage is to be scored, the number of targets and their type, the minimum number of rounds, the start position, and the condition the handgun is loaded. Competitors are also told how the time starts, whether it is a visual or audible start signal followed by the stage procedure. Commands used in practical shooting are as follows:

Load and make ready—Shooters may load their firearm only when given this specific command to load. The shooter is also given the opportunity to check and set their gear for the stage.

Are you ready?—No response is required, but many shooters nod or say yes, indicating they are ready.

Stand by—This command notifies the shooter to prepare for the start signal. After a short pause, the start signal will be issued.

Stop!—This is an emergency command at which the shooter must stop immediately. It is used in the event the course has not been set properly and the competitor must reshoot, if the shooter has violated a safety rule, or if there is an unsafe condition that requires the shooter to stop and unload.

If you are finished, unload and show clear—If the shooter is not finished, he or she has the option to continue firing. If finished, the competitor begins the unloading process.

If clear, hammer down and holster—It is *always* the shooter's responsibility to ensure that the firearm is clear while unloading. The range officer issues commands, but if the firearm is not clear and a shot is fired during unloading, the result is a match disqualification for the competitor.

Range is clear—The command notifying all competitors that the there are no loaded firearms on the range and that the range is safe.

Special categories and classifications based on ability level are recognized. Minimum requirements apply, but IPSC acknowledges individual, special categories. The official categories are Lady, Junior, Senior, and Super Senior. An international classification system establishes ability level by division in five classes: Grand Master, Master, A, B, C, and D class.

> **LINGO:** *Did you know that at many major IPSC regional events, at the end of the match there is usually a shoot-off? This is a man-vs.-man event where competitors shoot at an array of targets, usually steel, with either time or an overlapping steel target set to determine the winner. These events are very spectator-friendly and generate quite a crowd.*

There are several different divisions within IPSC. In the beginning there was only one division, and competitors shot in a heads-up format. As the guns and gear evolved and companies began research and development programs, things changed. The firearms used just one decade after the organization was formed were vastly different. Compensators were added to reduce felt recoil. Red dot optics were introduced to eliminate the need to line up the sights, and therefore competitors were able to shoot faster and more accurately on targets. As a result, everyday carry guns were no longer competitive, and the sport saw the need to develop divisions based on the types of firearms used.

Open

Open division has been dubbed the "race gun" division. This is the fastest division in IPSC, and the guns used feature compensators, optics, and high-capacity magazines. Typically shooters in Open post the fastest times on stages in a given event. Shooters have the most options and leeway to set up their rigs to best suit them within the rules. Common guns used in this division are high-capacity, single-action firearms in .38 Super, .38 Super Comp, and 9mm Major. The minimum power factor for Major is 160. There are no minimums for trigger pull weight and no maximums for handgun size or weight. Optical sights, compensators, and ports are all permitted. Magazines are limited to an overall length of 170mm.

Standard

In the Standard division a number of modifications are allowed. However, iron sights must be used, and optics, compensators, and porting are specifically prohibited. Essentially this is the iron-sight race gun division. Common firearms used in this division are high-capacity, single-action firearms in .40 caliber. The minimum power factor for major scoring is 170. A shooter's rig must be set up so that the firearm and all magazines are behind the point of the hip. Standard Division handguns with an empty magazine inserted must fit inside a box with the internal dimensions of 225mm x 150mm x 45mm. There is no maximum magazine length, however all magazines must be pass the box test as described above.

Modified

The Modified division is rather unique and was created to allow for highly customized firearms that are readily available internationally. Modified is a cross between Standard and Open. Optics, compensators, and porting are allowed, as they are in the Open Division. As in Standard, though, there is a 170 power factor floor for major scoring. Handguns must be worn behind the point of the hip, and firearms and magazines must also fit in the same 225mm x 150mm x 45mm box used for Standard firearms.

Production

This is a grassroots division that features the guns that are accessible through major manufacturers throughout the world. Firearms in this division are double-action, striker-fired, or double-action/single-action (DA/SA), and rules specifically state that the first shot attempted in a course must be double-action. There is also a minimum trigger pull weight of 5 pounds for the initial shot. All production guns are scored minor, so there is no advantage to shooting hot loads in this division. To be fair to all and not create a capacity issue for the division, all Production firearms are limited to fifteen rounds only. A shooter's rig must be set up so that the firearm and all magazines are behind the point of the hip. IPSC uses an approved list of firearms that have been deemed legal in the Production division. There is no box rule, but barrel length is limited to 127mm. Very few modifications are allowed, such as sights and the addition of grip tape. The guns cannot be permanently modified, and guidelines for external modifications are specifically listed in the rules.

Revolver

This division is reserved for revolvers only. The most commonly used firearm in this division is a Smith & Wesson revolver, the Model 625. The minimum power factor for major scoring is 170. Holster and ammunition carrier positions are not restricted to behind the point of the hip. There are no restrictions on trigger pull, handgun size, or weight, but competitors may only fire six rounds before reloading or face a procedural penalty.

LINGO: *Did you know that IPSC also has shotgun and rifle championships based on similar rules? In the past decade, action shooting sports have added long guns to the fun.*

International Practical Shooting Confederation (IPSC)

Sport Type: Action

Scoring: Points and Time

Targets: Paper and Steel

Competition Scope: Local, state, and regional events with premier national, continental and world championships.

Website: www.ipsc.org

Guns & Gear:
- ☑ Single Firearm Sport
- ☐ Multi-Gun Sport
- ☑ Additional Specialized Gear Required

Competition Results & Standings:
- ☑ Competitors are classified by ability level
- ☑ Competitors are classified by firearm modifications
- ☑ Special Categories are recognized

United States Practical Shooting Association (USPSA)

USPSA is the governing body for IPSC in the United States. Even though USPSA is a member of IPSC, the organization has developed additional rules, especially with regard to equipment for competitors in the U.S. Where IPSC has five divisions, USPSA has six. There are no set course requirements for USPSA matches as there are in IPSC with regard to stage size and the formula used for the number of stages in matches. Though there are several differences, USPSA and IPSC feature stages of fire that are constantly changing and test the shooter's ability to maneuver through a course of fire while shooting both fast and accurately. Many of the primary rules, especially with regard to safety and scoring, remain the same. Of the modern action shooting sports in the United States, USPSA has the most members. The sport has an extensive network of clubs participating at the local, state, regional, and national championships.

Including the classic target used exclusively in IPSC, USPSA events also use another paper target known as the metric target. The metric target is humanoid in shape and has four scoring zones. Courses of fire also commonly feature the use of pepper poppers, similar in shape to classic poppers in IPSC.

Different from IPSC, the minimum power factor in order to receive the benefits of major scoring in USPSA is set at 165 for all divisions. The minimum power factor for minor scoring is the same as IPSC at 125. Those that don't make major are scored minor. Ammunition that does not meet the minimum minor power factor floor results in equipment disqualification at the match.

The table on page 107 lists the point values for each target used in USPSA for both major and minor scoring.

	Classic	Metric
A Zone	5 Major / 5 Minor	5 Major / 5 Minor
B Zone		4 Major / 3 Minor
C Zone	4 Major / 3 Minor	4 Major / 3 Minor
D Zone	2 Major / 1 Minor	2 Major / 1 Minor

USPSA has four levels of matches. Level I represents club matches that are held at the local level throughout the year. Sectional and state matches that are conducted annually are Level II. The organization has divided the United States into eight areas, and Level III matches represent the annual Area Championships. The final level is the National Level, and for the past several years USPSA has either hosted single division national championships like the Single Stack Nationals or has combined divisions in a back-to-back national format. Specific round counts and the number of stages apply to each different level.

The special categories in IPSC (Lady, Junior, Senior, and Super Senior) are recognized, with the addition of Military and Law Enforcement. Like IPSC, USPSA uses classifier stages to establish ability classifications for shooters: Grand Master, Master, A, B, C, and D class.

In addition to the targets used in IPSC competition, USPSA allows the metric target with four scoring zones and a falling steel target called the pepper popper.

LINGO: *Did you know there is a website that specifically celebrates the women in practical shooting sports? WomenofUSPSA.com is dedicated to showcasing the diverse and talented women in the sport.*

There are six divisions in USPSA. Some are very similar to the divisions in IPSC, while others are vastly different. Regions within IPSC have some flexibility to create divisions and rule changes in order to accommodate firearms and specific laws within individual countries.

Open Division

As in Open in IPSC, guns in this division are highly modified and because of this, it is known as the fastest division. You'll see anything from red dot optics and custom work to firearms that include compensators and barrel and slide ports. There is no minimum trigger pull and no handgun size or weight restrictions. There is, however, a maximum magazine length of 171.25mm. This length extends beyond the mag well, and magazines in this division are often called "big sticks," holding more than 25 rounds. High capacity, single-action firearms in 9mm, .38 Super, or .38 Super Comp are commonly used in the Open Division.

Limited Division

Limited is most like the Standard Division in IPSC. The differences lie in magazine lengths and holster and mag pouch positioning. High-capacity .40 caliber handguns are most commonly used in this division to maximize major scoring and capacity. This is an iron-sight division, and optics and compensators are not allowed. There is no minimum trigger pull and no handgun size or weight restrictions. The maximum magazine length is 141.25mm for all magazines other than single-stack mags, in which 171.25mm is allowed. Internal modifications to improve reliability, accuracy, and function, as well as the exchange of minor components such as springs, safeties, and other small parts are permitted. External modifications or features designed to control or reduce recoil are specifically prohibited. USPSA uses an approved handgun list with a minimum factory production requirement of 500 units to establish guns legal for the Limited Division.

Limited 10

Limited 10 is a division that uses all the guns that are legal in Limited. However, there is a restriction on the number of rounds that can be loaded in any magazine used by the competitor on a stage. Competitors in this division can have no more than ten rounds in their magazines at soon as the stage starts. Unless otherwise specified, most courses allow shooters to start with one round loaded in the chamber and then ten rounds in the start magazine. This division was created due to the fact that some states have made the ownership of high-capacity magazines illegal.

Production

This is the grassroots, iron-sight division reserved for double-action and striker-fired handguns in USPSA, and only specific modifications are allowed. This division has several differences from Production in IPSC. Unlike in IPSC, there is no minimum trigger weight in USPSA Production, but USPSA does restrict the types of holsters that can be used. Holsters must be suitable for everyday use, with race gun holsters specifically prohibited, but both sports require that holsters and ammunition holders must be located behind the hip bone. Where IPSC limits production capacity to fifteen rounds in the magazine, USPSA limits magazines in this division to ten rounds. There is no major power factor in Production Division, and all competitors are scored minor. USPSA establishes a maximum size for the handguns and magazines in this division, and the firearm with an empty magazine inserted in the mag well must fit completely within a box with the internal dimensions of $8\,{}^{5}/_{16}$ inches x 6 inches x $1\,{}^{5}/_{8}$ inches. USPSA uses an approved handgun list, with a minimum factory production requirement of 2,000 units to establish guns legal for Production. There is a maximum weight that allows for 2 ounces with an empty magazine inserted over the weight listed on the approved pistol list.

Single Stack

Single Stack is a nostalgia, iron sight division with no compensators, barrel ports, or slide ports permitted. Using only metal-frame, single-stack 1911-style firearms, this division was developed due to interest in going back to the sport's roots. This division is similar to the Limited Division. The handgun with empty magazine inserted must fit completely within a box with the dimensions of $8\frac{5}{16}$ inches x 6 inches x $1\frac{5}{8}$ inches. Maximum rounds are loaded in magazines based on major or minor scoring. For major, competitors are allowed to load eight rounds. In minor, 10 rounds is the limit. There is a maximum weight of 43 ounces with the empty magazine. As in the Production Division, race gun holsters are specifically prohibited. Authorized and prohibited modifications are listed in the rule book.

Revolver

Another iron sight division where optical sights, compensators, and ports are not allowed, this division is most like IPSC's revolver division. There are no trigger pull minimums or maximum weight or size restrictions in this division. Race-style holsters are allowed. There is a maximum ammunition capacity of six rounds fired before the competitor is required to reload.

SCORECARD

United States Practical Shooting Association (USPSA) Handgun

Sport Type: Action

Scoring: Points and Time

Targets: Paper and Steel

Competition Scope: Local, state, and regional events with premier national championships.

Website: www.uspsa.org

Guns & Gear:
- ☑ Single Firearm Sport
- ☐ Multi-Gun Sport
- ☑ Additional Specialized Gear Required

Competition Results & Standings:
- ☑ Competitors are classified by ability level
- ☑ Competitors are classified by firearm modifications
- ☑ Special Categories are recognized

International Defensive Pistol Association (IDPA)

One of the youngest action shooting sports, IDPA was founded because a number of shooters were unable to convince practical shooting sports to return to what they considered the roots of practical shooting. A need for more practical, defensive courses and a sport where carry guns were competitive was recognized. At the time, USPSA had only Open and Limited divisions. Single stacks, double-action production guns, and revolvers didn't have a place to be competitive.

The founders of IDPA created a sport that they hoped would test an individual's shooting and gun handling skills, not the cost and modification of their equipment. Stages are called scenarios and simulate possible dangerous encounters and situations where handguns might be used in self-defense. Competitors are required to use any available cover at all times. To stress realistic shots in simulated self-defense situations, 75 percent of all shots must be from 15 yards or less. Shooter movement is also restricted to stress the use of cover, and at least 5 percent of all shots required in a match are to be fired on the move. There are limitations as to how far targets can be placed for one-handed shooting as well. Courses are also limited, in that no string of fire can exceed 18 rounds.

Similar safety rules to those in IPSC apply. Instead of a 90-degree muzzle safe indicator, IDPA establishes muzzle safe points for each course of fire. Unsafe gun handling and other potentially dangerous safety issues are not tolerated in the sport. Unlike most action shooting events that use cold ranges, IDPA events are sometimes conducted on hot ranges, based on host club rules.

IDPA is without a doubt the most subjective of all the action shooting sports. Fault lines are specifically prohibited. Instead, safety officers determine whether or not competitors are following the course procedure correctly and using cover efficiently. A shooter is considered to be behind suitable cover if 50 percent or more of the shooter's upper torso is behind a designated barrier. For low cover, the shooter's legs and feet must be completely behind cover, and one knee must be on the ground. A subjective penalty called a Failure to Do Right penalty of 20 seconds added to a shooter's total score can be assessed if a competitor attempts to circumvent the spirit or rationale of any stage. Other procedurals are issued in the event that a competitor violates the procedure as outlined in the course of fire description, resulting in a 3-second penalty per infraction.

In addition to firing shots from behind acceptable cover, competitors are required to carry their equipment concealed, using a garment like a vest or jacket that conceals the firearm. Holsters must be approved for competition and designed for concealed carry. Race- or competition-style holsters are specifically prohibited. Holsters must be worn on a standard belt that passed through belt loops and is no more than 1¾ inches wide. There are also rules about how close the holster can be from the belt and body. Like the holsters, ammunition carriers must also be worn on the belt and be suitable for concealed carry. The Velcro rig system pictured earlier in this chapter and used in other sports is not allowed in IDPA.

The range commands used in the sport are very similar to those used in IPSC. They begin with "load and make ready," "shooter ready," and "stand by." Once the competitor has completed the course of fire, the commands "slide forward or cylinder closed," "hammer down," "holster," and "range is safe" are issued.

In IPSC, courses of fire are designed to allow the shooter to solve the problem. In IDPA, shooters are given parameters on how they can shoot the stage, even the order they can shoot the targets. There are different types of target engagements unique to IDPA courses of fire. The first is tactical priority, which essentially means that targets must be engaged from near to far. In tactical sequence, every target must be engaged with one shot before they may be reengaged with however many shots are required on each target based on the stage procedure. Per the rule book, targets must be engaged in tactical priority at all times, unless tactical sequence is specified. "Slicing the pie" is a term used for shooting from behind cover. Targets are engaged in the order in which the shooter sees them. This minimizes exposure to targets the shooter has not shot.

The sport also designates acceptable reloads. There are tactical reloads, reloads with retention, and slide lock or emergency reloads. The only time you are permitted to leave a magazine behind and not on your person is in the event that it is empty. Tactical reloads and reloads with retention are reloads performed so that partially loaded magazines are always secured on the shooter. A tactical reload is one where the shooter retrieves a fresh magazine first, removes and captures the magazine in the gun, inserts the fresh mag, and then stows the used magazine. A reload with retention is one where the shooter removes the magazine from the gun, stows it, and then reloads with a fresh magazine. A slide lock reload is one where the magazine in the gun is empty and can be dropped on the ground without retaining it. Reloads can be initiated only while the shooter is behind cover.

Types of scoring in IDPA include Vickers Count and Limited Vickers Count. Vickers is like IPSC Comstock scoring, where shooters may fire as many shots as they wish. Limited Vickers is like Virginia Count, where the number shots permitted on the stage is limited to a specific number.

The official IDPA target must be used for all matches. The target is similar to a USPSA metric target in shape but uses different scoring rings. An 8-inch, round, down zero zone is centered in the upper chest area. The head area on the target is also a down zero zone. All other zones on the target have designated point values of -1 and -3. For each shot scored in a points down area, 0.5 second is added to a shooter's total time on a stage. Steel targets can be used in IDPA matches, but there are limits to the number of steel targets that can be used in courses of fire.

IDPA uses a paper target with scoring zones that result in .5 seconds added to a shooter's overall time for a stage.

No-shoot targets, called "nonthreats," are designated by hands on the target, simulating a surrender position. A 5-second penalty is assessed for a hit on a nonthreat target. In addition to scoring hits on the target, a "failure to neutralize" penalty is assessed in the event that a target does not have at least one hit in either the down zero or -1 zone. Hard and soft cover are also used to present shooting challenges.

IDPA is a trophy-only sport. Trophies are awarded to one out of every three shooters entered in a division or class. There are six ability classifications, based on match performance and score on the 90-round classifier, and they are Distinguished Master, Master, Expert, Sharpshooter, Marksman, and Novice. Special category awards are also issued to the high woman, law enforcement, senior, distinguished senior, junior, industry, military, military veteran, member of the press, international, and most accurate shooters.

In general, firearms in IDPA cannot have compensators of any type, add-on weights used for competitive advantage, disabled safeties or sights of a nonstandard configuration. There are five different divisions in the sport. In the pistol divisions, all firearms must fit in an IDPA test box measuring 8¾ inches x 6 inches x 1⅝ inches. High-capacity pistols can be used in some IDPA divisions, as long as they meet the requirements of the division and are not loaded beyond specified capacities.

IDPA uses the following divisions.

Stock Service Pistol (SSP)

A division for semiautomatic, double-action, DA/SA, or striker-fired firearms in 9mm or greater. The gun must fit in the IDPA test box with an empty magazine, and the maximum weight for this configuration is 39 ounces. The minimum power factor is 125. A division capacity of 10 rounds in the magazine plus one in the chamber of the firearm is designated for pistols this division. Lists of specific permitted and excluded modifications are included in the rule book.

Enhanced Service Pistol (ESP)

This is a division for semiautomatic pistols (the type of action is not restricted) in 9mm caliber or greater. The gun must fit in the IDPA test box with an empty magazine, and the maximum weight for this configuration is 43 ounces. The minimum power factor is 125. A division capacity of 10 rounds in the magazine plus one in the chamber of the firearm is allowed for pistols in this division. Lists of specific permitted and excluded modifications are included in the rule book.

Custom Defensive Pistol (CDP)

A division for semiautomatic pistols (the type of action is not restricted) caliber .45 ACP only. There is a minimum power factor of 165 for CDP. The gun must fit in the IDPA test box with an empty magazine, and the maximum weight for this configuration is 41 ounces. A division capacity of 8 rounds in the magazine plus one in the chamber of the firearm is allowed for pistols in this division. Lists of specific permitted and excluded modifications are included in the rule book.

Enhanced Service Revolver (ESR)

A division for revolvers in 9mm caliber or larger that safely meet a power factor of 165. Barrel length is limited to 4.2 inches or less. Speed loaders and moon clips are allowed in this division. Seven- and 8-shot revolvers can be used, but there is a stipulated division capacity of 6, requiring that competitors reload after firing 6 shots. Lists of specific permitted and excluded modifications are included in the rule book.

Stock Service Revolver (SSR)

A division for revolvers in .38 caliber or larger that use ammunition with a rimmed case. Barrel length is limited to 4.2 inches or less. Speed loaders can be use in this division, and moon clips are specifically prohibited. Ammunition in this division must only meet a power factor floor of 105. Seven- and 8-shot revolvers can be used, but there is a stipulated division capacity of 6, requiring that competitors reload after firing 6 shots. Lists of specific permitted and excluded modifications are included in the rule book.

LINGO: *Did you know there is also a back up gun division in IDPA? Used for side events and club matches only, back up guns must be a minimum of .32 auto or larger caliber. Barrel lengths are limited to 3.8 inches or less for semi-autos and 3 inches or less for revolvers. The total number of rounds that may be loaded into the handgun is five.*

SCORECARD

International Defensive Pistol Association (IDPA) Handgun

Sport Type: Action

Scoring: Time

Targets: Paper and Steel

Competition Scope: Local, state, and regional events with premier national and world championships.

Website: www.idpa.com

Guns & Gear:
- ☑ Single Firearm Sport
- ☐ Multi-Gun Sport
- ☑ Additional Specialized Gear Required

Competition Results & Standings:
- ☑ Competitors are classified by ability level
- ☑ Competitors are classified by firearm modifications
- ☑ Special Categories are recognized

International Confederation of Revolver Enthusiasts (ICORE)

The rule book states that ICORE is "dedicated to Wheel Gunners from every walk of life and for every purpose: from collectibles to competition." In developing their sport, ICORE has adopted ideas from several different shooting sports. At their premier annual event, the International Revolver Championships (IRC), competitors are tested in long, run-and-gun style courses of fire like those in USPSA and IPSC. There are also stages like those at the Steel Challenge, where competitors shoot strings of fire on steel targets, with one plate designated as a stop plate. Scoring is all time-based, and some courses dictate how you must shoot the stage, including target order, much as IDPA does. Finally, like the original NRA Bianchi Cup, ICORE uses the tombstone-shaped NRA D-1 target.

Target zones on the D-1 are designated as X, A, B, and C. There are no points allotted for hits on these targets. Instead, time is added to a competitor's total score based on where they hit each target. X and A zone hits add no extra time to a shooter's raw stage time. B zone hits add 1 second, and C zone hits add 2 seconds. A miss on a target is worth 5 seconds.

As in IPSC, no-shoots and hard/soft cover can be used to present different shooting challenges to the competitor. Each hit on a no-shoot target results in 5 seconds added to the shooter's score. Other procedural errors result in 5-second penalties as well. Overtime shots in courses that dictate the amount of time in the stage result in a 10-second penalty. A variety of steel targets can be used in events. Steel targets are scored as a simple hit or miss.

There are strict safety rules, as with all action shooting sports. Safety rules in IPSC generally apply, but ICORE uses different language in their rules to cover muzzle safety points. Instead of referring to this area as the 90 as in IPSC, ICORE describes muzzle safe

ICORE events use tombstone-shaped paper targets with scoring rings instead of using a point system like many other sports. For any shots scored outside the two centermost rings, time is directly added to a competitor's score.

zones as the 180. The 180 designates a 180-degree imaginary line that moves with a shooter throughout a course of fire that divides uprange from downrange. Any muzzle that breaks the 180 results in a disqualification.

In fact there are many similarities to IPSC. The range commands used in ICORE are the same as those used in IPSC, with the exception of the second-to-last command. Instead of "if clear, hammer down, holster" the command "if clear, close cylinder, holster" is used. Courses of fire are also similar. Courses in which no set time or maximum number of shots is dictated, called Comstock in IPSC, are referred to as Shots Unlimited in ICORE. When the number of shots is specified as with Virginia Count in IPSC, this is called Shots Limited.

All firearms used in ICORE must be .32 Magnum caliber or greater, revolvers only. There is no major power factor scoring, but there is a minimum power factor of 120. To encourage new shooters who may not have reloading equipment, the rule book lists specific factory ammunition permitted in matches that does not have to meet the power factor minimum.

As in IPSC, holsters and ammunition holders are attached to the belt, which must be worn at waist level. Women are permitted to wear their gun belts at hip bone level. The heel of the butt of the gun is not allowed below the bottom of the belt. There are no division-based restrictions on where holsters and ammunition holders can be placed, as long as the equipment and positioning are deemed safe.

There are six classifications based on ability level: Grand Master, Master, A, B, C, and D. Special categories are recognized for Junior, Lady, Senior, Senior Plus, and Law Enforcement. At the IRC, Six-Shooter and Snub Nose classes have also been recognized. Six-Shooter class designates any revolver with only six chambers in the cylinder. Snub nose is reserved for compact revolvers suitable for concealed carry.

There are just three divisions in ICORE: Open, Limited, and Classic.

Open

This division is for race revolvers. Compensators, venting, and ports are allowed. Open revolvers can have barrel and grip weights. Optics are allowed. Eight-shot revolvers using moon clips are most commonly used in this division.

Limited

Take away compensators, weights, and optics, and this is this is a revolver suitable for Limited Division. This is an iron-sight division and front and rear sights that extend beyond the muzzle are not allowed. Only unaltered factory or factory replacement barrels are authorized. Eight-shot revolvers using moon clips are most commonly used in this division.

Classic

Originally named "Retro," the Classic division features iron-sight revolvers legal in Limited, except that a Classic revolver can only have six chambers in the cylinder. Where moon clips are allowed in Open and Limited, only speed loaders can be used to reload in this division.

Handgun Action Shooting Sports » 123

International Confederation of Revolver Enthusiasts (ICORE)

Sport Type: Action

Scoring: Time

Targets: Paper and Steel

Competition Scope: Local, state, and regional events with premier world championships.

Website: www.icore.org

Guns & Gear:
- ✓ Single Firearm Sport
- ☐ Multi-Gun Sport
- ✓ Additional Specialized Gear Required

Competition Results & Standings:
- ✓ Competitors are classified by ability level
- ✓ Competitors are classified by firearm modifications
- ✓ Special Categories are recognized

Steel Challenge Shooting Association (SCSA)

Steel challenge is the purest form of speed shooting in the action shooting sports. It's all about how fast shooters can hit the steel targets. Even though the Steel Challenge has spanned three decades, the organization itself is young. It's only been in the past five years that there has been significant interest in growing the sport at the grassroots level. Some USPSA clubs will hold steel challenge events periodically throughout the year, and there are even some ranges that hold monthly matches. There are several regional events, state events, and even a national championship. There is definitely a movement to increase participation, especially for juniors. The Scholastic Steel Challenge program is a program that helps clubs and communities engage in steel shooting by promoting the sport to the next generation of competitors.

The main event is the Steel Challenge, an annual world championship that draws competitors from all over the globe. There are eight fixed courses of fire featuring targets as close as 7 yards all the way out to 35 yards. Targets range in size from 8-inch round plates to large 18 x 24 inch rectangular targets. On each stage there is a designated stop plate that literally stops the time when hit. Any targets that have not been successfully hit before the stop plate are assessed a 3-second miss penalty. Other penalties include 3 seconds for foot faults or creeping, moving to the gun before the audible start buzzer sounds. The maximum amount of time for a stage is set at 30 seconds and if a shooter fails to hit the stop plate, this is their automatic score for the stage.

Safety rules used in IPSC and USPSA are followed in SCSA competitions. There is no minimum power factor requirement, but all centerfire ammunition must be 9mm or larger and travel faster than 750 feet per second. In Rimfire events, only .22 long rifle ammunition is allowed.

Scoring is hit-based, and shooters are given the opportunity to complete five runs on each stage on all stages except for Outer Limits, where competitors shoot four runs. Unlike other action shooting sports where you only shoot a course once, Steel Challenge takes the shooter's top four (or three in the case of Outer Limits) fastest runs to compute overall scores. The fastest time in each division wins!

The range commands used are the same as those listed in the IPSC section above. The start position for all centerfire events is the "surrender position," with wrists above the shoulders. The start signal is audible and once it sounds off, the competitor can draw and engage the five targets of the stage. In Rimfire, shooters start with the firearm in hand, aimed at a designated point centered in front of the shooting position approximately twelve feet from the shooter.

There are no classifications in Steel Challenge, and all competitors shoot in heads-up competition against the clock. The sport is beginning to fully recognize special categories like Woman, Junior, Pre-Teen Junior, Senior, Distinguished Senior, and Law Enforcement.

There are many different divisions in SCSA, and the organization uses division rules for other sports. In addition to USPSA divisions, the sport also recognizes IDPA divisions and an Optical Revolver Division similar to ICORE's Open Division. There are also Rimfire Optic, Rimfire Iron, and Single Action Revolver divisions. It is common for competitors to enter more than one division in Steel Challenge, and a Steel Master title is awarded to the fastest time in an aggregate of Rimfire and two centerfire events. Most commonly, Steel Master is awarded to a shooter competing in Open, Rimfire Optic, and Limited or Production.

SCORECARD

Steel Challenge Shooting Association (SCSA)

Sport Type: Action

Scoring: Time

Targets: Steel

Competition Scope: Local, state, and regional events with premier national and world championships.

Website: www.steelchallenge.com

Guns & Gear:
- ✓ Single Firearm Sport
- ✓ Multi-Gun Sport
- ✓ Additional Specialized Gear Required

Competition Results & Standings:
- ☐ Competitors are classified by ability level
- ✓ Competitors are classified by firearm modifications
- ✓ Special Categories are recognized

NRA Action Pistol

The National Rifle Association's Action Pistol Program combines the classic skills of drawing from the holster and firing fast shots, accurately. Unlike the other sports that stress speed skills, in NRA Action Pistol all shots must be fired within specific times, and a competitor's score on the targets is what is reported in the standings. Action pistol is essentially an amped-up version of bull's-eye with reactionary targets and on some courses, the skill of transitioning from target to target. Unique to this action shooting event, a perfect score of 1920 and 192 Xs is attainable.

There are a number of different courses of fire listed in action pistol. In fact, there are 17 courses of fire total, however, state, regional, national, and world championships feature four main courses of fire, called events. They are the Practical, Barricade, Moving Target, and Falling Plate Events. The premier match of the action pistol season is without a doubt the action pistol national championships, the NRA Bianchi Cup.

There are six official targets in the Action Pistol rulebook, but only three are used at the Bianchi Cup. The NRA AP-1 is a tomb-

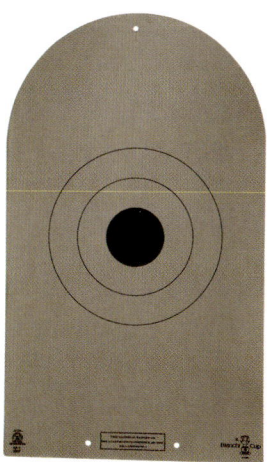

The NRA AP-1 is the official paper target used at the NRA Bianchi Cup. It has the same dimensions as the official target used in ICORE but features a solid black X-ring and visible black scoring rings.

stone-shaped paper target with four scoring rings located in the center. The X-ring is a black, 4-inch-diameter circle located in the direct center of the target and is worth 10 points and one X for each hit inside this scoring ring. The next scoring ring is the 10 ring, 8 inches in diameter. After the 10 Ring is the 12-inch 8 ring, named for the total of number of points awarded for hits in this scoring zone, 8 points. The remaining portion of the target is worth a total of 5 points.

Other targets used in the event are falling plates. These are 8-inch-diameter round steel targets that must be knocked down to score. One additional type of target is used in Bianchi for the Speed Event. This is another steel knock down target 28 inches high with a round plate 12 inches in diameter at the highest point of the target, essentially the same as the IPSC classic popper.

Each event at the Bianchi Cup includes a total of 48 shots with shots fired from four different yard lines. All strings of fire are timed, and shooters must complete all shots within the specified time frame, or misses and late shot penalties are assessed.

Practical Event

The competitor faces two targets set downrange with the tops of the targets set approximately 6 feet above the ground and 3 feet apart, edge to edge. Competitors may shoot from standing or prone at any yard line. The start position is standing with hands at shoulder height or higher. After the commands "Ready" and "Stand by," the targets turn to present to the shooter for the designated time allotted for each yard line and turn away from the shooter once the time has elapsed. The start is visual—there is no audible signal or buzzer. All shots can be fired with both hands except for the final string at the 10-yard line, where competitors must draw and transfer the firearm to their weak hand and fire with this hand only, without any support. The following is a breakdown at each yard line:

	String 1	String 2	String 3
10 yards	1 shot ea. Target, 3 sec.	2 shots ea. Target, 4 sec.	3 shots ea. Target, 8 sec (support hand only)
15 yards	1 shot ea. Target, 4 sec.	2 shots ea. Target, 5 sec.	3 shots ea. Target, 6 sec.
25 yards	1 shot ea. Target, 5 sec.	2 shots ea. Target, 6 sec.	3 shots ea. Target, 7 sec.
50 yards	1 shot ea. Target, 7 sec.	2 shots ea. Target, 10 sec.	3 shots ea. Target, 15 sec.

Barricade Event

A series of four barricades are lined up on the range in a row, one directly behind the other at each yard line. The barricades are 6 feet high and 2 feet wide. All shots must be fired in the standing position from within the shooting box, which is the width of the barricade and 3 feet long extending back from the bottom edge of the barricade. Two targets are set up downrange, centered behind the barricades center line and set at total of 6 feet apart, edge to edge. The start position is standing in the barricade with the palms of both hands on the face of the barricade. This is another visual start event, and competitors must remain in the start position until the targets turn to face them before they can draw and engage the targets. All competitors may use the barricade for support, but in all divisions except the Open Division, no portion of the firearm can touch the barricade for any shot. The following is a breakdown at each yard line:

	String 1	String 2
10 yards	6 shots on 1 target (either right or left) in 5 sec.	6 shots on the remaining target (either right or left) in 5 sec.
15 yards	6 shots on 1 target (either right or left) in 6 sec.	6 shots on the remaining target (either right or left) in 6 sec.
20 yards	6 shots on 1 target (either right or left) in 7 sec.	6 shots on the remaining target (either right or left) in 7 sec.
25 yards	6 shots on 1 target (either right or left) in 8 sec.	6 shots on the remaining target (either right or left) in 8 sec.

Moving Target

Shooting boxes 3 feet by 3 feet centered in front of the moving target range, set the stage for the Moving Target event. All shots must be fired from the standing position. The start position is hands at least shoulder high, and this is another visual start stage. Once the shooter assumes the ready position, the target appears from behind a wall or barricade and moves from the right to the left side of the range, traveling 60 feet in 6 seconds. The competitor may then draw and fire the required number of shots on the target before it disappears behind a wall or barricade. The shooter repeats the start position, and the same target then moves from left to right. At the close distances, the 10- and 15- yard lines, the competitor fires 6-shot strings. At the back two distances, the 20- and 25-yard lines, the shooter fires 3-shot strings. The following is a breakdown at each yard line:

	String 1	String 2	String 3	String 4
10 yards	6 shots, target moves right to left	6 shots, target moves left to right		
15 yards	6 shots, target moves right to left	6 shots, target moves left to right		

	String 1	String 2	String 3	String 4
20 yards	3 shots, target moves right to left	3 shots, target moves left to right	3 shots, target moves right to left	3 shots, target moves left to right
25 yards	3 shots, target moves right to left	3 shots, target moves left to right	3 shots, target moves right to left	3 shots, target moves left to right

One important note for this event is that the competitor has a total of 7½ minutes to complete this entire course. The time starts from the moment they enter the shooting box until the start of the last ring of fire.

Because the target moves quickly, to be successful in the Moving Target Event, shooters must aim ahead of the target's center in order to hit the center at different distances. This is called leading the target. In the Open Division, shooters use custom optics and optic bases that are zeroed for the appropriate lead. In Metallic and Production, it's very common for people to simply hold their sight picture on different areas of the target, leading the target to ensure their bullets impact in the center. In order to determine lead for this event, it is necessary to know the speed that your bullets are traveling in feet per second. With the moving target traveling 10 feet per second (fps), use the following formula:

(distance to target in feet divided by bullet velocity in fps) x target speed in inches per second = amount of lead in inches

10 yards	(30 ft / bullet velocity in fps) x 120 in per sec.
15 yards	(45 ft / bullet velocity in fps) x 120 in per sec.
20 yards	(60 ft / bullet velocity in fps) x 120 in per sec.
25 yards	(75 ft / bullet velocity in fps) x 120 in per sec.

Plate Event

There are no scoring rings on the plates and therefore this event carries the greatest disaster factor in Action Pistol. This is because shooters either hit their targets and score 10 points each or they are assessed misses, resulting in zero points added to their score. There are four strings of fire, and competitors shoot a series of 6, 8-inch plates placed 1 foot apart from edge-to-edge, 4 feet above ground level two times each from each yard line. The start position is standing with hands held at least shoulder high. Unlike the other events, the plates feature an audible start. Once the commands "Ready" and "Stand by" are given, competitors listen for the audible buzzer, either a whistle or horn, that indicates when they can draw from the holster. Plates lock in place at the Bianchi Cup so that once the time limit has expired on a given string, the plates will not fall even when hit. The following is a breakdown at each yard line:

	String 1	String 2
10 yards	6 plates in 6 sec.	6 plates in 6 sec.
15 yards	6 plates in 7 sec.	6 plates in 7 sec.
20 yards	6 plates in 8 sec.	6 plates in 8 sec.
25 yards	6 plates in 9 sec.	6 plates in 9 sec.

After all scores are computed for the four main events, the top finishers in each category and division compete in the Speed Event, a spectator-friendly event held before the final awards ceremony. After initial qualifiers are fired, the field is narrowed down even more, and the top shooters compete in a man-vs.-man shoot off on banks of five falling steel targets set at 10 yards. The fastest shooter wins!

As with most NRA sports, there are a number of special categories and individual national records are up for grabs. All five classifications of the NRA classification system are used—High

Master, Master, Expert, Sharpshooter, and Marksman. This is the only action shooting event eligible for the NRA's Distinguished program.

> **Tip:** *Unlike many other action sports, if your unloaded firearm is accidentally knocked out of your holster in NRA Action Pistol the result is a match disqualification. Consider keeping your firearm bagged or in a case until you are ready to report to your stage to shoot to reduce the chances of being DQ'd.*

Historically at the Bianchi Cup, four firearms divisions have been recognized. There are no weight restrictions on firearms, but for all handguns, the trigger pull weight cannot be less than 2 pounds except for the Production Division, which has heavier trigger weight requirements. The minimum caliber is 9mm, and the minimum power factor is 120.

Open

This division is the "anything goes" division and features semiautomatic firearms and revolvers with optics, compensators, and even "wings." Attached to the sides of the gun, wings are used to help Open Division shooters mount their firearms directly to the face of the barricade on the Barricade Event. This feature allows for ultimate stability and perfect scores on the stage to be fired.

Open Modified

Another division that features compensated firearms with optics, but wings are specifically prohibited. This division has not been recognized in recent Bianchi Cup competitions.

Metallic

This is an iron-sight division, and semiautos are restricted to 6.25 inches in barrel length with a maximum sight radius of no more than 8.5 inches. For revolvers, barrel length is limited to $8^5/_8$ inches and sight radius to 11 inches. Compensators, optics, and wings are specifically prohibited in this division.

Production

The grassroots division of the sport, the Production Division has seen the most growth within the action shooting sports across the board. In Action Pistol, a firearm must be a semiautomatic handgun or revolver that is in a manufacturer's catalog and has been readily available to the public. Only post and notch sights are allowed in this division. Custom shop firearms are specifically prohibited, and the division represents the guns that are found at local gun shops. Holsters are also restricted to carry-type holsters, with race holsters specifically not allowed.

This is a double-action or striker-fired division, so no single-action handguns are allowed, and minimum trigger weight rules apply, which include a 3.5-pound first shot minimum trigger pull regardless of firearm type. Barrel length is limited to 5.35 inches for semiautos and 6 inches for revolvers. Visible internal and external modifications are prohibited except for those specifically listed in the rule book. Some of these modifications allow for grip texturing enhancements like checkering or stippling and specific changes to the firearm's sights. Replacement barrels are allowed, and other specific modifications are also allowed, providing no cuts to the firearms are required.

> **TIP:** *In Action Pistol competitions you can expect to have your gun inspected and trigger weighed at Match Registration and at any point in the competition. Always make sure your firearm meets safety and division requirements.*

NRA Action Pistol

Sport Type: Action

Scoring: Points

Targets: Paper and Steel

Competition Scope: Local, state, and regional events with premier national and world championships.

Website: www.nrahq.org/compete/actionpistol.asp

Guns & Gear:
- ✓ Single Firearm Sport
- ✓ Multi-Gun Sport
- ✓ Additional Specialized Gear Required

Competition Results & Standings:
- ✓ Competitors are classified by ability level
- ✓ Competitors are classified by firearm modifications
- ✓ Special Categories are recognized

Chapter 9

MULTI-GUN

Multi-gun sports offer all the fun with more than one gun! Though some sports allow you to compete in more than one division and with more than one firearm, compiling scores as an aggregate as in Steel Challenge and Bianchi Cup, multi-gun competition generally refers to using more than one gun to count toward the total event score. In NRA Conventional Pistol, competitors use multiple handguns to complete the course of fire in centerfire, rimfire, and .45 caliber. In action shooting, multi-gun events use a combination of rifle, pistol, and shotgun during stages. The sport is often referred to as 3-Gun.

Multi-gun action shooting has evolved over the past two decades. Matches in the 1990s incorporated rifle and shotgun side events for aggregate titles. Renegade matches that had no affiliation with shooting sports organizations ran successful tournaments for years. Cowboy action shooters have incorporated rifle, shotgun, and pistol into their championships as well. Now more than ever, though, the sport of multi-gun has grown in popularity, even spawning television shows dedicated to the sport.

IPSC, USPSA, and IDPA all have their own rules for competitions. Add to that the number of premier events that aren't sanctioned, and you have a sport that can be somewhat confusing to get into. Each event in the circuit has its own flavor, and the stages at each competition directly reflect the layout of each range.

Contestant on History Channel's Top Shot Season 2 and two-time Ladies Open National Champion at the USPSA Multi-Gun Nationals, Maggie Reese enjoys the challenge of competing with several guns in one course of fire.

Some events feature intense rifle accuracy at long distances. Others are more physically demanding, requiring shooters to maneuver through long courses on foot. In multi-gun matches, stages generally use two or more firearms in a course, though some can be dedicated to just one firearm, and others use all three.

Multi-gun competitions can be gear-intensive and shooters can expect to carry rifle, pistol and shotgun ammunition on their rig. A Safariland ELS rig like the one pictured here allows the shooter to customize their mag and shell holder positions for each stage. Photo by Stephen McKelvain.

The greatest challenge in getting started is learning the rules for each competition. Though the organizations I mentioned above have specific rules, some of the most popular events run their own rules and are not affiliated with any organization. There has been a movement for all popular competitions to use the same rules, brought together by the online resource, www.3gunnation.com, which has created a 3-Gun Nation match series with substantial prize money on the line. If you decide to compete in a multi-gun event, be sure to contact match officials and ask them the rules for that particular competition. This information may or may not be easy to find or readily available on the event's website.

Scoring in most multi-gun events is time-based. Time is added to a competitor's overall score on a stage for failing to hit targets based on the competition rules. Target values can vary. This means that some targets can be worth more than others, and failing to hit higher-value targets results in more time penalties added to the competitor's score.

Because shooters can begin a course carrying one or more firearms, special rules are in place for competitors to leave firearms throughout a given stage. The term used in the USPSA rulebook is "abandoned." Guns can be abandoned in designated areas, safe zones, or retention devices and, if they are unloaded, in a safe condition. These rules allow the shooter to draw or pick up their other firearms and complete the course safely. Depending on the event, some allow loaded firearms to be abandoned in designated areas as long as all safeties are activated. Others require the firearm be unloaded completely before abandoning.

Multi-gun is gear-intensive. Competition rigs are set up so that magazine pouches, shell holders, and holsters can be changed and moved around to maximize performance on a stage. Add three guns to the mix, and all this gear can certainly add up. You'll also need a good way to haul all your gear around. Shooters use either specially designed bags or carts to move firearms and equipment from stage to stage.

> **TIP:** *Because multi-gun events are physically demanding, requiring shooters to engage targets from standing, kneeling, and prone positions, consider investing in elbow and knee pads, and always wear long pants while competing.*

There are three main divisions in multi-gun: Open, Limited, and Tactical. Not all events call the divisions by these names, which can add to the confusion. Firearms are categorized into division by firearm modifications, most specifically caliber, and use of optics. Following are the details for each division, but be sure to check with each event's administrators to make sure you have equipment suitable for the division you wish to compete in.

Open

This is the race gun division of multi-gun, and optics are allowed on all firearms. For rifles, compensators, porting, and bipods are all allowed. There is no limit to the number of rounds in a magazine. More the one optic can be mounted to the rifle. The Open shotgun can have a compensator, porting, and optics. Shooters can load ten shells in the magazine plus one in the chamber to start a course, and speed loaders are popular. Pistols are often high-capacity, using extended magazines and optics.

Limited

Limited division is a mostly iron-sight division, with optics allowed only on the rifle. For rifle, shooters can use a nonmagnified optic, usually a red dot electronic sight. Compensators are restricted to specific dimensions, and bipods are not allowed. Shotguns must be stock as well, with no compensators or porting. Shooters are limited to loading eight shells, plus one in the chamber, at the start. Pistols must use iron sights. High-capacity firearms are popular, but magazines are limited in overall length.

Tactical Optics

Much as in the Limited division, optics are limited to the rifle. The rifle can have only one optic. Compensators are restricted to specific dimensions, and bipods are not allowed. Shotguns must be stock as well, with no compensators or porting. Shooters are limited to loading eight shells, plus one in the chamber at the start. As in Limited, pistols are restricted to iron sights, and most shooters compete with high-capacity firearms using magazines limited in overall length.

Heavy Metal

The Heavy Metal divisions feature major power loads and large calibers. There can be round restrictions of twenty rounds for rifles. The rifle must be .308 caliber or larger. In Heavy Metal Limited, only pump-action shotguns can be used, and a minimum power factor of 165 must be achieved in .45 caliber or larger for the handgun. For Heavy Metal Tactical, any shotgun action is allowed, and pistols in this division must be .40 caliber or larger. The 165 power factor minimum also applies. All pistols in Heavy Metal, both Limited and Tactical, are limited to ten rounds loaded in the magazine.

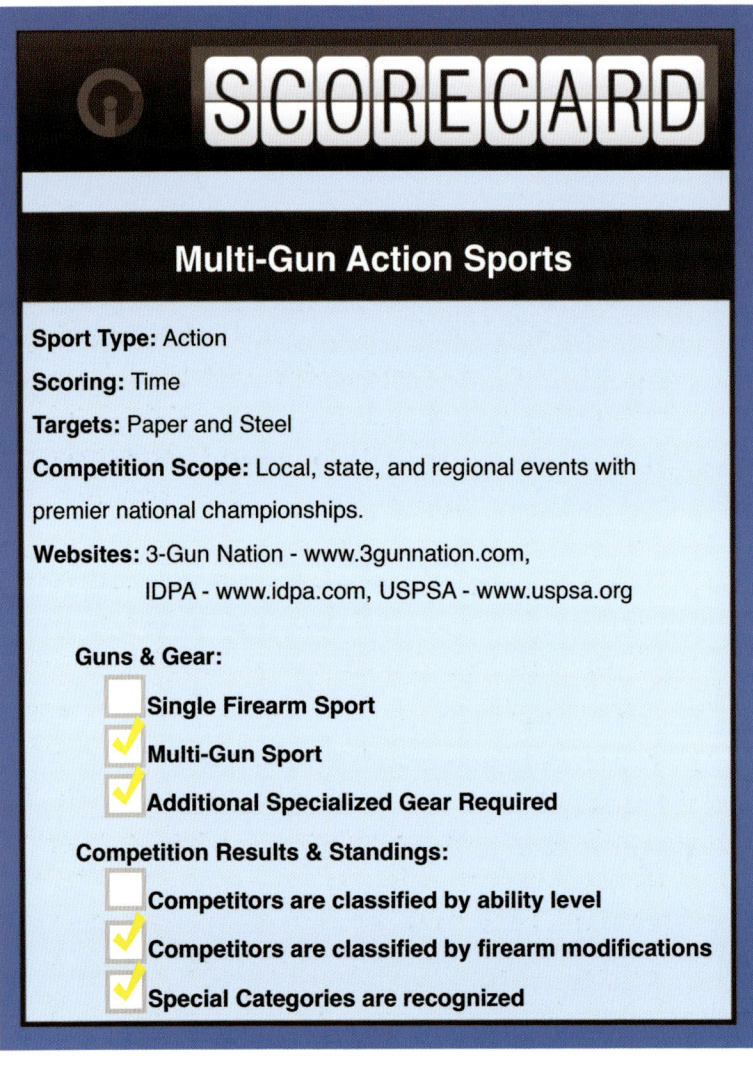

Chapter 10»

NOSTALGIA SHOOTING SPORTS

Love spaghetti westerns? Was history your favorite subject to study in school? Do you enjoy role-playing, or perhaps have a passion for fashion? If so, then the nostalgia shooting sports are a great way to incorporate these interests with fun shooting competitions. These sports feature guns and gear from specific periods. Originals and replicas can be used, but any modifications are subject to the sport-specific rules.

There are a number of shooting sports that feature nostalgic firearms. Costuming can also determine whether or not you can compete in these events. The newly formed American Zoot Shooters Association (www.zootshooters.com) showcases the guns and gear of the Roaring Twenties. This multi-gun sport requires shooters to dress in clothing of the period, and as in many action shooting events, shooters compete against the clock, engaging a variety of targets.

The National Muzzle Loading Rifle Association (NMLRA) is dedicated to the sport of muzzleloading and to muzzleloader enthusiasts. The NMLRA promotes the muzzleloading heritage through historical reenactments, exhibits, museums, libraries, and other related programs. There are also several organized competitions, and the NMLRA works closely with the National Rifle Association (NRA) to promote this type of shooting. The NRA National Muzzle Loading Championships has even been held in conjunction with the NMLRA events.

Other sports also feature blackpowder events or divisions. The NRA Black Powder Target Rifle events test shooters' skills with rifles that exclusively use blackpowder, as well as blackpowder events like the cowboy action SASS Black Powder Shootout. Blackpowder tends to burn slowly and produces a significant amount of smoke, unlike modern smokeless or semi-smokeless powders. Follow through (in

Kenda Lenseigne participates in one of the fastest-growing equestrian sports in the United States, cowboy mounted shooting. She holds six world records and is the only woman to have won the Overall World Championship, beating both male and female competitors to earn this prestigious title.

this case, keeping the sights on target even after the trigger is pulled) is extremely important in these events.

By far the most popular nostalgia shooting sports are those of the cowboy variety. Cowboy action shooting sports feature the guns and dress from the American Cowboy era. SASS and Mounted Cowboy Shooting are two popular cowboy action shooting sports.

Single Action Shooting Society (SASS)

SASS is one of the largest shooting organizations in the world, and its members are dedicated to preserving the history of the Old West. Members are required to select an alias or cowboy name and also wear period costuming to further develop their characters at SASS events. Competitors can compete in a match's main event, as well as in side matches and team competitions. SASS recognizes shooting categories based upon age, gender, costuming, equipment, shooting style, and/or propellant.

Shooters use only single-action firearms, both originals and replicas. Handguns must be holstered except when the shooter is actually firing them, and ammunition used in any course of fire must be carried on the shooter in a bandolier or cartridge or shotshell carrier, unless otherwise specified. This gear must be of traditional design, in keeping with SASS objectives. There is a minimum and maximum power factor for ammunition used.

SASS is an action-based shooting sport. At each stage, competitors race against the clock, engaging reactionary steel targets of varying size and difficulty. The time it takes a competitor to complete the stage, minus any penalties for missed targets, is the shooter's score for that course. Having fast reflexes and the ability to manipulate a number of firearms and are critical skills in order to perform at the top. Times are added for all the stages, and this number represents the competitor's total score in the event. The fastest time wins!

SCORECARD

Single Action Shooting Society (SASS)

Sport Type: Action/Nostalgia

Scoring: Time

Targets: Steel

Competition Scope: Local, state, and regional events with premier national and world championships.

Website: www.sassnet.com

Guns & Gear:
- ✓ Single Firearm Sport
- ✓ Multi-Gun Sport
- ✓ Additional Specialized Gear Required

Competition Results & Standings:
- ☐ Competitors are classified by ability level
- ✓ Competitors are classified by firearm modifications
- ✓ Special Categories are recognized

Mounted Shooting

Mounted shooting combines the excitement of drawing a single-action revolver and shooting reactionary targets, all from the back of a horse. It is also one of the fastest-growing equestrian sports in the United States. Mounted shooting events can be as exciting as attending a rodeo and have elements reminiscent of Wild West exhibition shows. Competitors wear two single-action revolvers loaded with five rounds each of blackpowder blanks. Blanks are commonly loaded in firearms used in Hollywood movies for action scenes. These blanks have sufficient power to burst balloons, the targets used in mounted shooting competitions. Some events even incorporate shooting rifles from the back of a horse.

There are two primary organizations for mounted shooting: SASS Mounted Shooting, a sub-organization of the Single Action Shooting Society, and the Cowboy Mounted Shooting Association (CMSA). Both require Western clothing and Western holsters and belts. Matches are often held in arenas, much like rodeos, and are spectator-friendly. Riders are timed through each course fire. Misses accrue penalties, resulting in seconds added to the competitor's raw time. The contestant who rides the fastest and hits the most targets wins!

SCORECARD

Mounted Cowboy Shooting

Sport Type: Action/Nostalgia

Scoring: Time

Targets: Balloons

Competition Scope: Local, state, and regional events with premier national and world championships.

Websites: CMSA - www.cowboymountedshooting.com
SASS - www.sassnet.com/mounted_news.php

Guns & Gear:
- [ ] Single Firearm Sport
- [x] Multi-Gun Sport
- [x] Additional Specialized Gear Required

Competition Results & Standings:
- [x] Competitors are classified by ability level
- [ ] Competitors are classified by firearm modifications
- [x] Special Categories are recognized

Chapter 11 »

TAKING THE PLUNGE

With so many shooting sports, it can be hard to decide where to get started. The sports covered in this book represent only some of the competitions out there—there are certainly plenty more, with new events showing up on match calendars frequently. Maybe one of the sports featured in this book left an impression on you, but if you still aren't sure, here are some things to consider, as well as some additional information you should know before competing in your first shooting event.

Investment

You may not have a whole lot of disposable income to invest substantial dollars in a shooting sport. There are definitely programs out there that can help you learn about shooting and give you an idea if it's something you will enjoy. As I mentioned in Chapter 3, Women & Shooting, the NSSF's First Shots program is an excellent way to give shooting a try without spending a significant amount of money. Participants have the opportunity to learn from qualified instructors about local and state laws and have the chance to learn the fundamentals of shooting.

Several shooting sports accommodate new shooters by providing divisions that require less financial investment. A new competitor certainly has the option of purchasing high-end equipment should they wish to jump right in. I find that shooting sports can be related to going for a ride in a car. You can certainly get from point A to B in a reliable, comfortable vehicle, or you can do so in the latest and greatest four-wheel-drive SUV with leather interior and all the bells and whistles. No matter what you are driving, though, the view along the way is the same.

Shotgun sports are very popular because new shooters can show up to a shotgun event with a gun purchased at a sporting goods store or local dealer and a couple of boxes of shells. Certainly there are high-end, specialized shotguns that are designed for specific purposes, but as an initial investment, these are not necessary.

Most action shooting sports have iron-sight divisions in which guns that can be purchased at local gun shops can be competitive.

Rimfire divisions like Steel Challenge offer a way for people to compete without investing a significant amount of money in sport-specific gear.

Production or stock divisions allow for guns that aren't highly modified to compete heads up against one another. Some events, like the Steel Challenge, even have a rimfire division. No holster is required—all you need is a .22 caliber handgun, magazines, ammunition, eye and ear protection, and a suitable bag to put it all in.

For precision sports, it gets a bit tricky because these sports have specific firearm requirements and allowable modifications. Precision silhouette shooting uses hit/miss scoring that is easy to understand, and there are no holsters or highly specialized gear required. The gun is the most significant investment. For other precision-based events, additional gear like shooting jackets, gloves, spotting scopes, etc., though helpful for top performance, are not required to compete. If you enjoy the challenge in precision sports, there are options to further specialize and even upgrade equipment to help shooters become more competitive.

The Value of Going to an Event

You may have seen shows on television or have watched or read about competitions on the Internet. Most shooting sports have associated websites, and there are certainly a number of videos on the Web, but the best way to get an idea of what to expect is to attend a competition as a spectator first. Find an event in your area, make sure you pack eye and ear protection, and go check it out.

When you arrive, it's best to let the event administrators know that you are there. Most ranges have clubhouses or areas designated for competitors to register and pay for an event. Introduce yourself as someone interested in giving the sport a try. You may need to sign a release waiver in order to watch the event. Be sure to ask if there is anything you should know, especially with regard to safety, before heading out to watch the action.

Don't be afraid to take notes. There are a number of things you should pay attention to so that you are prepared to shoot your first match. Here's a list you can copy and take with you:

- How do people transport their firearms?
- When and where are competitors allowed to handle firearms?
- When and where are competitors allowed to handle ammunition?
- What do people commonly wear, both for clothing and footwear?
- How are shooters organized, i.e., squads, lanes, relays, etc.?
- What range commands are used?
- How is the event scored and reset for each competitor?
- How long does the event take from start to finish?
- Is the event outside or indoors?
- If outdoors, what is the terrain?
- Are food and water available for purchase?
- Is there an orientation program for new competitors?

People often get caught up in the excitement of attending their first match and forget to pay attention to the logistical details that will help prepare them for competition. Answering these questions will help you decide everything, from your wardrobe to water and snacks to bring with you.

How to Prepare for Your First Competition

No matter what sport you try, there are some things you will want to do to prepare yourself for competition. The most important thing is to understand firearm safety. Being safe is what is going to allow you to have a successful first-time experience at a shooting competition. No matter the event, never point your firearm in an unsafe direction. Becoming familiar with sport-specific safety rules, as well as any specific range safety rules is important. Firearm safety is completely your responsibility. Take your time. Even if you are competing in a timed event, never rush when it comes to handling your firearm.

You should also learn your firearm's controls before you shoot. Know how to work all the safeties and how to load and unload your firearm. Become familiar with the manual controls like the magazine release, bolt release, slide stop, pump or lever action, etc.

Practice your fundamentals in dry fire. To dry fire, you first must ensure that you have no ammunition loaded in the gun or in any loading devices. In fact, it's best not to have any ammunition around you at all. The act of dry firing is going through the motions of shooting "dry," without ammo. Make sure that it is safe to dry fire your firearm. Some firearms, especially rimfire guns, may require a dry-fire plug or snap caps to prevent parts breakage. Dry fire allows you to work on your stance, grip, sight alignment, sight picture, and trigger control off the range, even in the comfort of your own home.

Taking a good dry fire shot (*No ammo!*)

- Assume a proper shooting stance or position for your sport.
- Acquire a proper grip on your firearm.
- Perform any action to the gun to set the trigger so that a dry-fire shot can be fired, i.e., pull back the bolt, slide, hammer, etc.

Snap caps are usually made of plastic and are the exact size and shape of your ammunition, but cannot be fired.

- Place the sights on target.
- While keeping the sights on target, apply smooth pressure to the trigger until the dry-fire shot breaks.

If you are competing in a sport that requires advanced gun handling skills, you can practice these in dry fire as well. Drawing the firearm from a holster, picking the firearm up from a table, reloading with empty magazines, transitioning from target to target, and transferring the gun from hand to hand are just some of the skills you can practice without any ammunition.

Your First Competition

What to Bring

Regardless what sport you decide to compete in, you'll want to make sure you bring items you need to compete with and those that will help you stay comfortable. Here's a checklist similar to what I use to pack for every match I shoot in:

☑ **Gear Checklist**
☐ Firearm with case
☐ Shooting bag or kit
☐ Ammunition
☐ Magazines, speed loaders, etc.
☐ Optic/spotting scope
☐ Water
☐ Snacks
☐ First aid kit
☐ Sunscreen
☐ Bug repellent
☐ Lip balm
☐ Ear protection
☐ Eye protection

- ☐ Compact tools (Allen wrenches, screwdrivers, and any tools that might help me in the event that I need to disassemble my firearm)
- ☐ Lubricant or gun oil
- ☐ Small cleaning kit with gun cleaner, brush, cotton swabs, and rag
- ☐ Spare batteries for any electronic equipment
- ☐ D-Lead or hand wipes
- ☐ Notepad with pen
- ☐ Sport-specific shooting gear—jacket, gloves, pants, shoes, mat, rig
- ☐ Outdoor gear
- ☐ Outerwear (cold, warm, and/or wet weather gear)
- ☐ Hat with a brim
- ☐ Appropriate footwear
- ☐ Umbrella
- ☐ Portable chair
- ☐ Camera or video camera

What to Expect

When you arrive, make sure you check in at the registration desk and complete any equipment checks. Let the match administration know you are new and that it is your first competition. If there is an orientation program, arrive in time to attend. Some clubs may even have liaisons to help and guide you in your first match. Take advantage of any program like this. Be sure to let the individual match officials on the line know that you are new. This will help them assist you through the course of fire.

Most ranges welcome new shooters with open arms. The belief is, the more shooters the better! You may run into a handful of people who may not want to compete with a new shooter. Don't be offended. These individuals may wish to compete only with a set group of friends or may be training for a major event, trying to replicate the intensity of high-level competition. Try not to take it personally—just focus on being safe and having fun.

You can expect to be nervous. You can expect to be excited. You can expect to be a little scared. That's all normal! You may feel some pressure to perform well. Your number one goal for your first match is to simply be safe. Don't worry about your score or where you place in the results. Accept that you are new and that you are ready to have a great time. Follow all range officer, safety officer, or referee instructions, and never be afraid to ask a question if you are confused, especially when it comes to being safe.

> **TIP:** *Ask to shoot last or on the final relay. This will give you the opportunity to watch other shooters compete and help you relax.*

Chapter 12 »

FUNDAMENTALS

The first step in learning how to become a good shooter is to make sure you have a strong foundation. Firearms instructors often teach four basic skills in shooting. They are stance, grip, sight alignment, and trigger control. Of the four, sight alignment and trigger control are the most universal throughout different sports, though there are certainly sport-specific idiosyncrasies that come into play. Grip and stance can vary depending on the firearm—whether it is a handgun, rifle, or shotgun you are shooting.

Stance

Finding a stance that allows you to shoot the best and replicating it is critical in precision shootings sports and those that require shooting a series of shots on a single target. Because the goal is to shoot the most accurate shot, every time, you will want to develop a stance that you can both assume easily and one that provides the steadiest platform from which to shoot. Seek out coaching or explore ways to make modifications to your precision shooting stance to maximize your performance.

In precision events like the one pictured here, where members of the U.S. Armed Forces compete at the Interservice Pistol Championships, shooters have fine-tuned their stance to deliver the best results on target. Photo courtesy of the U.S. Army Marksmanship Unit Public Affairs.

In sports where the shooter and/or the target moves, the proper two-handed shooting stance is one that allows for control of recoil and allows you to acquire targets easily. Start facing your target and place your feet shoulder width apart. If you are right-handed, you will want to move your right foot back slightly. For left-handed shooters, move the left foot back. As a general rule, the more the gun recoils, the more you'll need to broaden your stance

by moving your feet wider apart. The lighter you are, the less mass you have behind the gun, and using a wider stance will also help you to control recoil better.

Next, you will want to bend your knees slightly, similar to how a boxer would stand in a boxing ring. By bending the knees, the boxer's body is positioned to absorb hits in much the same way a shooter can counteract the effects of recoil. Finally, bend slightly forward at the

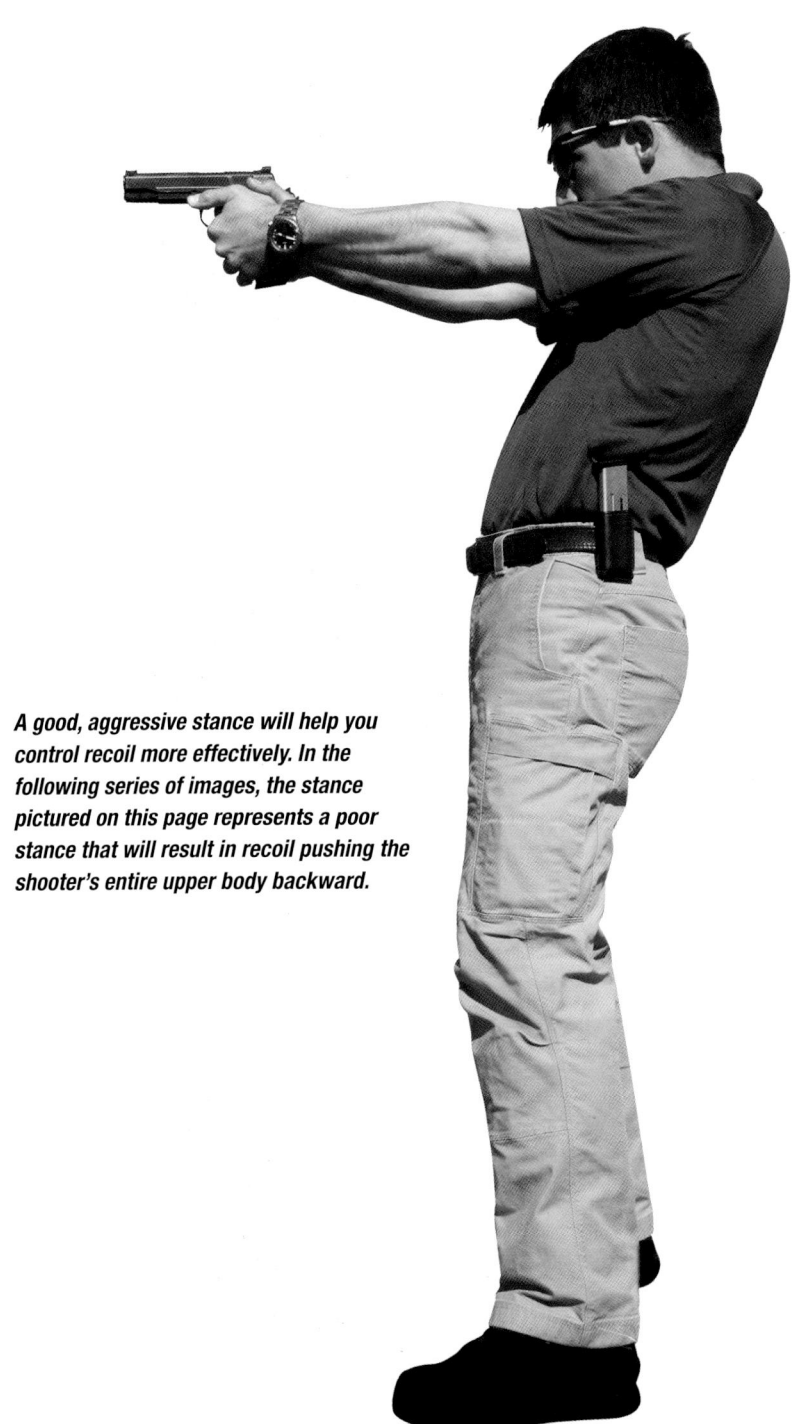

A good, aggressive stance will help you control recoil more effectively. In the following series of images, the stance pictured on this page represents a poor stance that will result in recoil pushing the shooter's entire upper body backward.

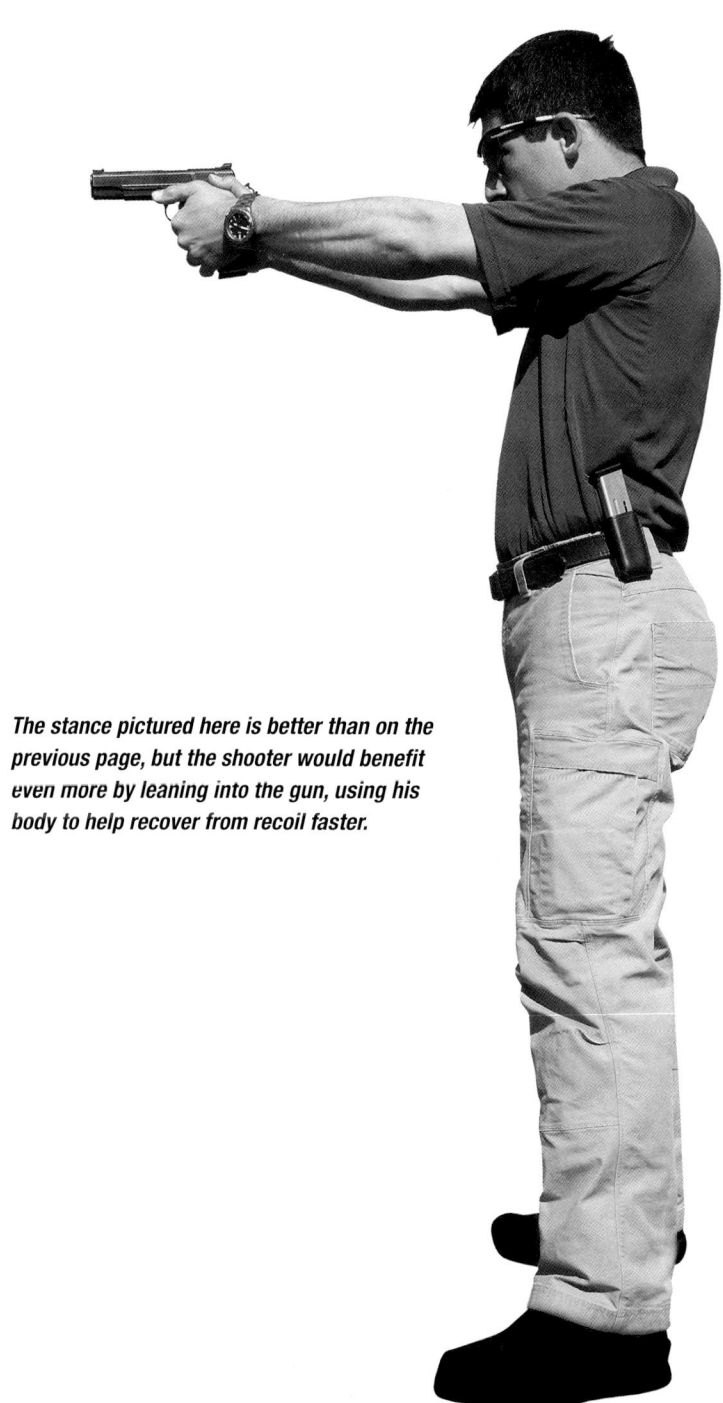

The stance pictured here is better than on the previous page, but the shooter would benefit even more by leaning into the gun, using his body to help recover from recoil faster.

Example of a good shooting stance.

waist. Shooting a larger caliber? Lean into the gun even more. In this position your body acts as a shock absorber, being able to control the recoil much more than if you were standing stiff and erect.

Oftentimes new shooters stand fully erect with feet close together while leaning back slightly instead of leaning into the gun. Shooting from this position will only make it more difficult to hold the gun up for long periods of time. It is also a difficult stance to maintain because recoil causes the shooter to lean continually farther and farther back with every shot.

Depending on whether you're shooting a rifle, shotgun, or pistol, the basic stance and position of your feet can vary slightly. A rifle that may not have as much recoil does not require as aggressive a stance as a shotgun. Moving the feet wider apart and moving the strong-side foot back farther while bending at the waist allows the shooter to use the body to help recover faster after each shot. Generally, the more a gun recoils, the more aggressive and wider the stance.

When shooting a handgun, how you position your arms is also important. Most shooters in the action shooting sports use what is referred to as the Isosceles Position. An isosceles triangle is one where two legs of the triangle have the same length. An Isosceles Position of the arms is similar to that of an isosceles triangle. You may have heard of the Weaver Position, or even other types of push/pull techniques. These do work to help control recoil, but an added benefit of the Isosceles Position is that you can both control recoil and have the ability to transition the gun from target to target faster, especially when targets are set wide apart. The best action shooters in the world use the Isosceles Position to compete and win.

Form an isosceles triangle with your two arms, and with your chest forming the base of the triangle. Keep elbows high and slightly bent. In much the same way that you bend your knees in your stance, keeping your elbows bent in this position will help you control recoil and allow fast target-to-target transitions. Another benefit to keeping your elbows bent is reducing the wear-and-tear effect recoil can have on elbow joints over time.

This photo series shows examples of good stance with a rifle and a shotgun, based on the recoil power of the firearms and the size of the shooter.

The Isosceles Position is one where the shooter's arms and chest form an isosceles triangle. This is a preferred arm position for those competing in the action shooting sports, as it allows for both efficient recoil control and the ability to move the gun faster on wide target transitions.

There may be occasions in action shooting sports when you will be required to shoot with one hand. Some courses of fire may challenge you to shoot with either your strong or your support hand. Other courses may require that you carry an object in one hand while you shoot. Having an aggressive stance is helpful in controlling recoil when shooting with one hand.

LINGO: *The support hand is your nondominant hand. For right-handed shooters, this is your left hand. For left-handed shooters, this is your right hand. In many sports this is referred to as the weak hand.*

For one-handed shooting with the strong hand, your standard shooting stance might work for you. You may wish to have an even broader stance though, so that your support-side foot is forward of your strong-side foot. In the event that you are required to shoot support hand only, switch your feet so that your nondominant foot is ahead of your strong-side foot. When possible, place your nonfiring hand on or near your chest. This will keep your nonfiring hand from becoming an issue during a shot and also puts it close to the gun should you need to transfer or manipulate the firearm.

Finally, think of your shooting stance as your foundation. Oftentimes stance is overlooked because shooters focus on grip, sight alignment, and trigger control. Remember, a good stance gives you the steady platform from which to shoot.

Grip

Once you have established a good stance, getting a good grip on the gun is important. Your hands control all aspects of the firearm, and how you position them is important to ensure you shoot both safely and efficiently.

For long guns, the first step is to position the butt of the stock into the point where your arm meets your chest on your strong side—this is known as the pocket of your shoulder. Study the rifle and shotgun images in this chapter. You want to avoid placing the gun on your

In one-handed shooting, changing foot position in the stance can help a shooter control recoil more effectively.

arm or the shoulder itself, especially if you are shooting a firearm with heavy recoil. The firing hand is placed either on the pistol grip or the stock so that you can both grip the firearm and access the trigger with your index finger. The support hand grasps the stock and helps the strong hand to push the gun into the shoulder pocket. The support hand also serves as a directional guide, adjusting the gun left to right as necessary.

For handgun shooting, the grip can vary between semiautos and revolvers. Unlike long gun shooting, where so much of the body is used to control recoil, with handguns, grip can become critical when controlling recoil and recovering from a shot. The best grip is one that allows the shooter to fire an accurate shot and recover to shoot the next shot as necessary.

Semiauto Pistols

Eye dominance (see page 180) is not an issue with handgun shooting, and therefore it is best to shoot with your dominant hand and use your nondominant hand for support when shooting with two hands. The easiest way to get a proper grip is to think of your contact points. The first is on the back of the gun with your strong hand. Make a V with this hand. That low point of the V in the web of your hand is where you will want to make contact high on the back of the grip of your handgun. The higher your grip, the better you will be able to control recoil. Once you seat the web of your hand onto the back of the grip, wrap your fingers around the front, keeping your thumb high.

The next step is to bring the support hand into the picture. Near the second joint of your index finger is where you will want to make contact with the bottom of the trigger guard. Wrap the fingers of your support hand around your strong-hand fingers and mate the base of your support hand to your strong hand. Your support hand will be canted forward. The bone located at the base of support hand should nestle right into the angle created by your strong hand, found

A good semiauto pistol grip is one where the hands fit together, eliminating any open spaces.

right at the base of the thumb where it meets your hand. It may feel slightly uncomfortable to grip the gun this way. If you have ever gripped a golf club properly, it probably felt uncomfortable and a bit foreign at first too. But by filling in all the gaps, this method will help prevent the firearm from moving around in your grip.

◉ **Tip:** *By keeping your thumbs pointing forward in a good two-handed grip, you can think of your thumbs as a gross form of sight picture, thrusting them toward the target as your eyes find the sights.*

⚠ *SAFETY CONCERN – When gripping a semiauto pistol, do not place the thumb of your support hand so that it rides along the top of your strong hand, behind the firearm's slide. If you fire with your support hand in this position, when the slide moves to the rear you could become injured!*

Revolvers

Some shooters use the same grip described above when shooting a revolver. If you decide this will work for you, it is very important to remember to keep your thumbs away from the moving cylinder to prevent potential injury. Another very popular way to grip a revolver that helps eliminate risk is the thumb-over-thumb technique. With this grip, the thumb of the support hand hooks over the thumb of the strong hand.

Just how strongly should you grip a handgun? Many instructors will suggest a 60/40 technique. In this case, 40 percent of the grip strength comes from the strong hand and 60 percent comes from the support hand. For me, applying these proportions is far too complicated and is just one more thing to think about. When I'm shooting I want to focus on acquiring the sights, getting a good sight picture, and working the trigger properly, not what percentage of my grip strength I am applying to the gun. This is further complicated because, as a woman, I find that my hands are not as strong as those of some of my male competitors. When I grip a handgun in the action shooting sports, I grip it as strongly as possible while still being able to move my trigger finger freely.

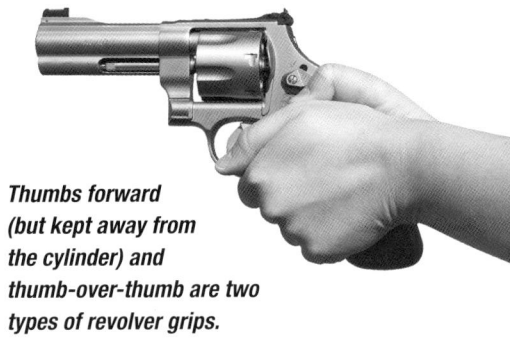

Thumbs forward (but kept away from the cylinder) and thumb-over-thumb are two types of revolver grips.

Instead of getting caught up in how much I should grip

the gun, I focus on the key areas of grip contact. I use my support-hand fingers to pinch the front of the grip, squeezing my strong-hand fingers into the gun. The second area of grip contact I pay attention to is at the back of the grip. I used my chest muscles to press my hands together at the back of the gun to help me compensate for any lack of hand strength I might have.

Finally, how much the gun recoils will also dictate how much grip pressure you should apply. If firing a soft-shooting .22 caliber handgun, you don't need to apply your superhuman grip strength. If you're shooting hot loads through a large-caliber handgun, like a .44 Magnum, the stronger your grip, the better you will be able to control recoil.

Sight Alignment

LINGO: *Post and notch, fiber optic, tritium, peep, ghost ring, and serrated are all terms used to describe different site configurations and features.*

Sight alignment is the process of centering the front sight into the rear sight in order to acquire proper sight picture on a target. If you're using optics, this ends up being very simple. Just place the crosshairs or red dot on target and you are ready to shoot. With post and notch sights, you have to line up the front and the rear sight to make a precise shot. When extended out on target, the front sight post should rest in the notch of the rear sight. There

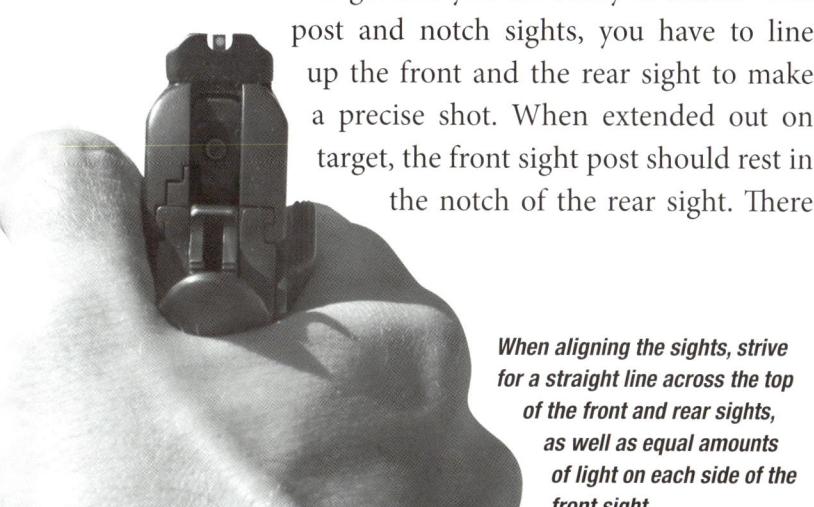

When aligning the sights, strive for a straight line across the top of the front and rear sights, as well as equal amounts of light on each side of the front sight.

should be equal amounts of light on either side of the front sight. Line up the top four corners created by the front and rear site. You should be able to draw a line straight across the top of your sights.

Peep or ghost ring sights use a dot and ring system. With these sights, center the top portion of the front sight in the center of the circle or peep hole. Keep in mind that these sights may not be legal for stock divisions in some shooting sports.

Changing out the iron sights on your firearm is one way to personalize it. Two types of rear sights are fixed and adjustable. Fixed sights are fitted to the gun, and when an adjustment is needed for windage, they must be physically moved to the right or left using tools. With adjustable sights, the ability to move the sight is built into the design. The shooter can make easy changes to windage and/or elevation with a simple turn of a screwdriver. Which is better? It's a matter of personal preference. For precision sports, adjustable sights are most common. For speed shooting and guns used for self-defense, fixed sights, like the Warren Tactical Sights in the sight alignment photo shown on the previous page, are often preferred because fine adjustments are not needed and they are less likely to break.

Zeroing is a term used by shooters to describe the process of coordinating sight picture (point of aim) with the desired point of impact. Some shooters, especially those in precision-based shooting sports, sight in their guns to hit with a noncenter hold. These shooters find that it is easier to aim in another location on the target instead of trying to find the direct center. An example of this is a 6 o'clock hold, where the gun is zeroed to hit the center of the target when held at the 6 o'clock position, or base, of a bull's-eye target. This is all a matter of personal preference. Regardless of where you hold, it is important to aim at a very specific location with every shot.

For precision shooting sports, you want the most perfect sight picture possible. Arc of movement (AOM) is the premise that, regardless of how steadily you hold a sight picture, you will see the sights move. Everyone has an arc of movement, though experienced precision shooters are known to have very small AOMs. Though your AOM may seem dramatic, keep in mind that the muzzle of the gun is actually moving very little. Don't be alarmed. Accept that you will see the sights move. If you apply smooth and consistent trigger control, the bullet will impact where you want it to on target.

In action shooting sports, acquiring the sights quickly is very important, and a center hold is the preferred way to zero your firearm. Think of the area just above the front sight as where you want your bullet to go. Because you will not have the option to adjust your sight for every shot, it is very important to know exactly where you will hit targets at varying distances. Ammunition can also change where rounds impact. It's a good idea to check your zero at several yardages that you anticipate shooting so that you can plan your sight picture placement accordingly. Zero for the most common, average distance you will likely engage targets. Adjust where you aim for targets at distances where you see your impact change.

Within the action shooting sports, because everything is based on a specific amount of time or how fast you shoot a course, the center zone on a target tends to be much larger than in the precision sports. Because of this, your acceptable sight picture is much broader. With speed as a factor, you can be slightly off in your sight picture, but still score an acceptable hit on target.

Trigger Control

You're in the proper stance, have a good grip, and the sights are lined up on target. Now it's time to press the trigger. Proper trigger control is crucial in precision shooting sports. Pulling or yanking on the trigger too hard can result in a shot that ends up being low and left. Think of proper trigger control as if you are dragging your trigger finger through thick peanut butter, all in one smooth motion. Whether you perform this motion slowly, taking as much time as necessary, or do so rapidly, executing proper trigger control will help ensure your shot hits precisely where you see your sights before the shot breaks.

> **LINGO:** *Squeezing the trigger or pressing the trigger are other terms used to help shooters visualize proper trigger technique.*

Some shooting sports don't require excellent trigger control. Shotgun shooters are known to slap the trigger as soon as they are ready to shoot. Because of their ability to follow through with a shot, trigger control isn't so critical. In action shooting sports, easy targets at close distances don't usually require excellent trigger control in order to score center hits.

Oftentimes shooters diagnose poor shots on target as the result of poor trigger control. Sometimes the error may not lie in how you squeezed the trigger, but rather moving the gun at the moment right before the shot breaks. Shots that impact extremely high could be a case of simply anticipating the shot, not improper trigger engagement. By anticipating the shot, the shooter is actually forcing the gun to perform mock recoil before the shooter has completely squeezed the trigger. Shots that are extremely low could indicate the shooter is anticipating the effect of the recoil by countering and pulling the gun low before the shot is fired. Anticipating the shot can result in missing a target completely. Apply good trigger control technique, holding the sights on target until the shot breaks in order to get the best results.

What Else Should You Know?

There are a few more things beyond stance, grip, sight alignment, and trigger control that are also considered shooting basics. Eye dominance and breathing are two factors that affect your performance as a shooter.

Eye Dominance

Eye dominance can become a significant issue for some shooting sports. Basically everyone has a dominant eye, and ideally that is the one you want to use when looking at the sights. There are two easy ways to determine which eye is dominant. For both methods, you will want to define a target. This can be a small picture frame or even a light switch on the wall. The target should be small and at least 10 feet away.

The first method is to place one hand over the other so that you form a small triangle. Think of the triangle as your viewfinder. Keeping your hands in this position, extend them so that you can see your target through the viewing hole created by your hands. Now, slowly bring your hands toward your face, keeping the target constantly in view. You'll notice that your hands will automatically move toward one eye. The eye you end up seeing the target with is your dominant eye.

The second method uses the same target. Take one hand and point at your target with your index finger with both eyes open. Close your right eye. Now open it. Close your left eye. Your index finger will shift off target when you close one of your eyes. Whichever eye does not cause your finger to move off target is your dominant eye.

Eye dominance is not so critical in handgun shooting or any sport where you can close or block sight for one eye. It can become an issue when a shooter finds that he or she is cross-dominant. This means that the shooter's strong-hand side is not the same side as their dominant eye. There are a couple of simple fixes. The first is simply forcing the nondominant eye to do the work. Simply closing the eye—or purchasing a blinder for the dominant eye designed to block the view of the sights—can achieve this. Another simple fix is to place a piece of frosted tape in front of the dominant eye's line of sight. This prevents any problems with getting a proper sight picture but still allows for maximum peripheral vision.

One way to determine eye dominance is to form a triangle with your hands and keep them in this position as you move them toward your face.

Eye dominance can be determined by pointing your index finger toward a target and closing one eye at a time. A shift in where your finger appears to point with one eye closed indicates your nondominant eye.

In two-handed handgun sports, another simple fix is to turn your head so that the dominant eye can do its work. For a cross-dominant shooter who is right-handed but left eye dominant, the firearm stays in the strong hand, but the shooter turns the face slightly to the right so that the left eye lines up with the sights. Cross-dominant shooters can also move the gun over so that they can align the sights with their dominant eye.

Where cross-dominance can be most challenging is in long gun shooting. Because the shooter's face is so close to the sights with the cheek pressed to the stock, simply moving the head in some firing positions is not an option. In some cases blinders may work, or the shooter can simply close one eye. For some, shooting with the nondominant hand is the best way to go, especially in precision sports or those where time is not a significant factor. In other long gun sports where gun handling skills are critical, this might not be ideal, due to the fact that some may find using their nondominant hand in this way is inefficient and too challenging.

> **TIP:** *Should you shoot with one eye or both eyes open? If you can see with your sights clearly with both eyes open, this is the way to go. If not, try squinting with one eye or using frosted tape on your shooting glasses.*

Breathing

Breathing is very important in all shooting, but it is not the same for all shooting sports. In sports that are not precision based, the important thing to remember is to breathe. Breathe naturally, at will, based on what action you are performing. Holding your breath for an entire stage in an action pistol match might mean that you could pass out—and that's definitely not a good thing!

Precision shooting sports are all about controlling everything that can be controlled. Breathing is definitely something to take into consideration when taking a precise shot. If you have a very long time to shoot a shot, you want to make sure that your breathing cycle doesn't affect where the bullet impacts on target. Hold your strong hand out front of you as if you were aiming on a target, and watch the top of your hand. Now breathe in deeply, and exhale. You should see your hand move up and down. Now imagine if you had a pistol in your hand. The difference could mean your sights move completely off target in some sports! Learning how to control your breathing and taking a shot at the best point in time is referred to as breath control. In precision courses, most shooters find that inhaling deeply and controlling the exhale while taking the shot works best for them. The shooter stops the breath on the exhale, taking a respiratory pause to begin to squeeze or press the trigger.

A solid foundation of basic skills is necessary to become a good shooter. Working on fundamentals isn't just for beginners, though. The best shooters know that constant work to improve these skills only results in better shooting performance.

Chapter 13 »

ADVANCED SKILLS

You've competed in your first match and you are officially hooked! Now it's time to work on the techniques and skills that will help you improve. You may wish to take a class or find a coach. Shooting instruction isn't something you are likely to find in the Yellow Pages. Ask your fellow competitors for recommendations. The Internet is also an excellent resource. Because of the wealth of blogs, videos, and other websites, keep in mind that you will want to thoroughly research any training before pursuing it.

Another excellent resource is the NRA's *Shooting Sports USA* magazine (SSUSA). SSUSA is a free online publication and offers a wealth of information on NRA-sanctioned shooting sports as well as other shooting events. The magazine frequently covers information and tips that pertain to becoming a better shooter within the NRA shooting disciplines. Sign up for free issues of SSUSA at nrapublications.org/ssusa.

Universal to all shooting sports, one area you can work on is trigger control. Precision, action, and shotgun events all require a press of the trigger in order to execute a successful shot. Dry fire is an excellent, inexpensive way to learn the best trigger control for your sport.

In stationary sports, learning the best position to shoot from is the next step to improving your score. Whether you are standing, sitting, kneeling, or shooting from prone, a good position provides the foundation for a shot. Adjusting your position may be uncomfortable at first. Your shooting position shouldn't be painful though, as this may limit your ability to shoot well. Any change will take time to implement, and this is where having a coach can be extremely helpful and cut down on your learning time.

In precision sports, pure shooting skill is tested. With the goal to hit the target in the center as many times as possible, shooters develop a specific shot plan for every shot. Consistency is the key. The shot plan is a mental checklist shooters use to ensure they have a good position and grip. Once the sights are on target shooters take into account their breathing cycle and use words or mental imagery to apply techniques that will help them execute perfect trigger control. Once the shot is fired, the shooter applies successful follow through to bring the sights back on target.

Outdoor precision sports, especially long-range events, often involve taking weather conditions into account. An advanced skill for shooters in these sports is learning how to account for any wind that might affect the impact of the bullet. Watching wind flags and reading any mirage—a wavy illusion that appears before targets—become valuable skills for extreme accuracy.

In clay target shooting, learning how to position your body for each type of target or shot can help you improve your score. Training your eyes to pick up a target as soon as it appears will help you react quicker and will help you acquire the clay faster and ultimately improve your chances of making a good shot. Perfecting gun motion for both tracking the target and follow through will also help you place higher in the standings.

Nostalgia sports represent the widest variety of shooting skills, and some sports are precision-based while others focus on speed. For the precision-based sports, working on positions, fundamentals, and perfecting your equipment is critical to improving as a shooter. For others like Single Action Shooting Society (SASS), many of the action shooting skills listed below will apply. In any speed-oriented event, working on improving reaction speed and hand-eye coordination is beneficial.

For action shooting events, there are a number of ways you can improve your overall performance. Isolating techniques and training them individually is the first step. Putting these skills together in a stage is what truly separates the best performers from the rest. There are so many skills beyond just shooting in the action shooting sports. Here are some of the most common that are tested on the clock.

Draw

Most action shooting sports require drawing from a holster. Where you can position your holster and what type of holster you can use are sport- and division-specific. Regardless of where your hands must be in the start position, the first step to a successful draw is getting to the gun. In these sports it is most common to have either an audible or visual start signal. The very moment you hear or see the start is when you want to launch into action.

> **TIP:** *In audible starts, listen for the very first tone of the buzzer. Don't wait for the entire buzzer to sound before you move. This will help you achieve a faster draw and improve your twitch reflexes.*

Regardless of what position your hands are in at the start signal, both hands should start moving at the same time. The support hand moves to the area between your chest and belly button. It should be open and ready to receive the handgun. Your strong hand should come down onto the grip of the gun in the holster. The web of the hand should be positioned high on the back of the grip so that when you do draw, you already have the beginnings of a good grip. Next, wrap the fingers around the gun and make sure that you have a grip that will allow you to control the firearm and not drop it. If at this point your grip doesn't feel right, it's best to try to fix it right then and there.

⚠️ *Dropping a loaded firearm in competition is dangerous and will result in a disqualification for unsafe gun handling.*

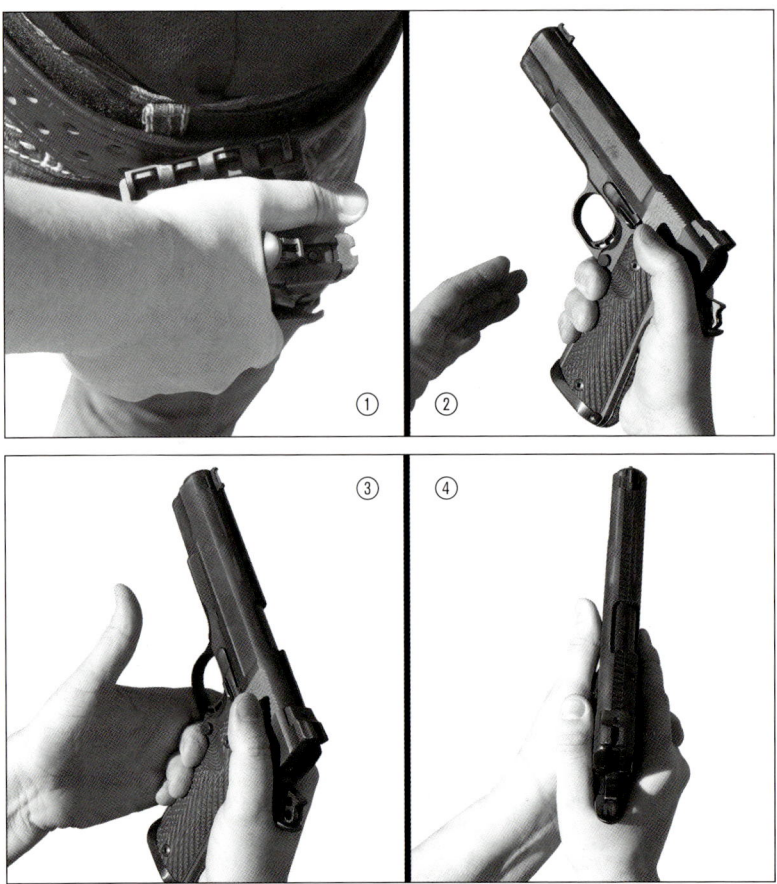

A good draw starts with getting a firm, high grip on the gun. The series of photos above shows that the support hand is open and ready to receive the gun. Once the support hand is in position on the gun, the shooter can extend the arms out on target.

Next, draw the gun out of the holster, keeping the muzzle pointed in a safe direction and the trigger finger straight and outside the trigger guard. As your gun hand meets your support hand, the gun's barrel should be somewhat parallel to the ground. The support hand wraps around the gun and strong hand in a proper two-handed grip.

At this point you can begin to place your trigger finger inside the trigger guard. If you are shooting a very heavy, double-action trigger you can even begin to start the initial press of the trigger. This is called prepping the trigger, and the purpose is to take up the initial portion of the trigger pull as you come on target. Prepping the trigger allows for just the last portion of the trigger to be pressed as soon as you are on target and makes for a faster shot. It's important to note that you should prep the trigger *only* if you have safe control over the firearm with the muzzle pointed downrange at the target. Dry fire is an excellent way to learn how to prep your trigger. If you have a light trigger or are not comfortable with prepping the trigger, you can begin to place your finger inside the trigger guard, but do not place your finger on the trigger until you are ready to shoot.

When you're extending the handgun out on target, your eyes should be focused on your target. As you move the gun into firing position, your front sight will appear in your peripheral vision. As you continue to move, the front sight will appear on the target, with the rear sight moving up into place to cradle the front sight. If you are shooting a handgun with an optic, you'll see the top of the optic on target, and as you move the gun into position, the target will appear through the lens. Make any necessary sight picture adjustments at this time and apply proper trigger control to take the shot.

One-Hand Draws & Transfers

Another type of draw is a strong-hand-only draw. If possible, begin in a good strong-hand shooting stance (see Chapter 12, Fundamentals). At the start signal, go through the same motions you would for two-handed shooting, except at the point where your support hand would meet your strong hand to extend out on target, bring your support hand into your chest and extend out with one hand only. The stronger the recoil, the wider your stance and the more aggressively you may need to lean into the gun.

In some action shooting courses of fire, you may be required to draw and transfer the gun to your support hand. In order to execute a safe transfer, always remember to keep all fingers out of the trigger guard at all times. If possible, start in a good, aggressive shooting stance. At the signal, move your hands the same as you would for a standard draw.

Before transferring the gun to the support hand you will have to draw it from the holster with your strong hand. There are two ways to grasp the gun with the strong hand. The first is as you would for any draw, acquiring a full grip on the pistol. The other is where the shooter grasps the bottom two-thirds of the pistol grip, leaving just the upper portion of the grip exposed. Instead of the support hand being open and ready to acquire a two-handed grip as you would when shooting with both hands, your support hand should be open and ready to accept the pistol. If you prefer to grasp the same way for all draws with a full grip, keep control of the firearm with the strong hand, but as your support hand comes in contact with the gun the back portion of your strong hand at the base of the thumb moves away from the grip, allowing your support hand to move into place. If you prefer the two-thirds grip method, simply insert the web of your support hand between your strong hand and the upper portion of the grip and onto the back of the gun. In both methods, as you move the strong hand away, the support hand replaces it. *Never* toss or throw the handgun into the other hand. When transferring the gun from hand to hand, there should always be constant contact on the firearm at all times.

The key to safe support-hand transfers is *control*. You need to maintain control of the firearm with at least one hand at all times. The other critical thing to remember during this type of transfer is to

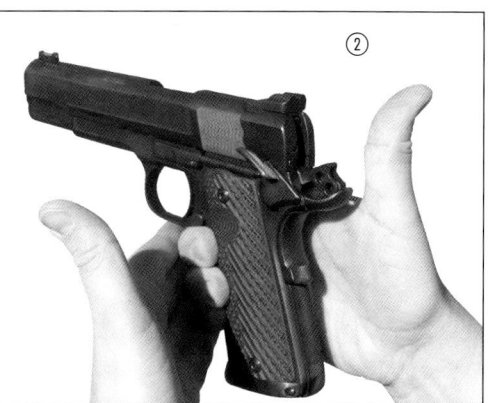
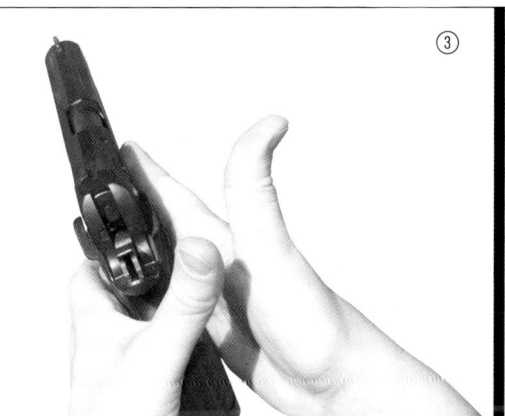
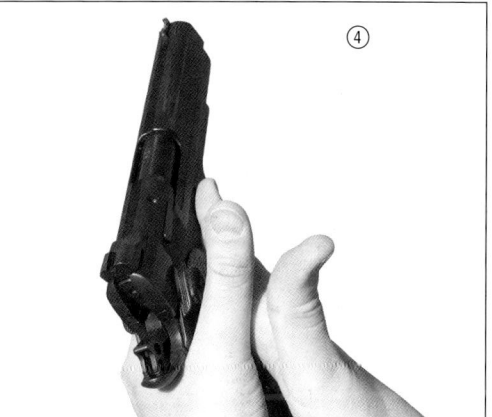

Support-Hand Transfer—Standard Strong-Hand Grip

The two sets of photos on these pages show the shooter's view of a support-hand transfer. The series above shows the use of a standard grip with the strong hand. The images on page 191 show another view of a transfer using the two-thirds grip method.

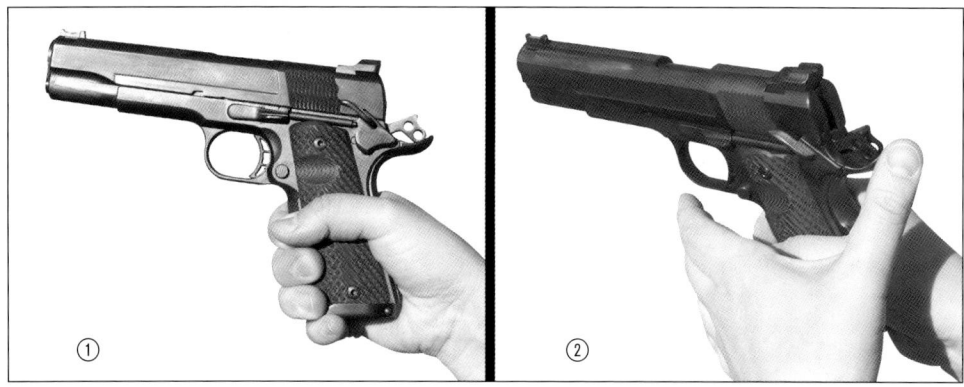

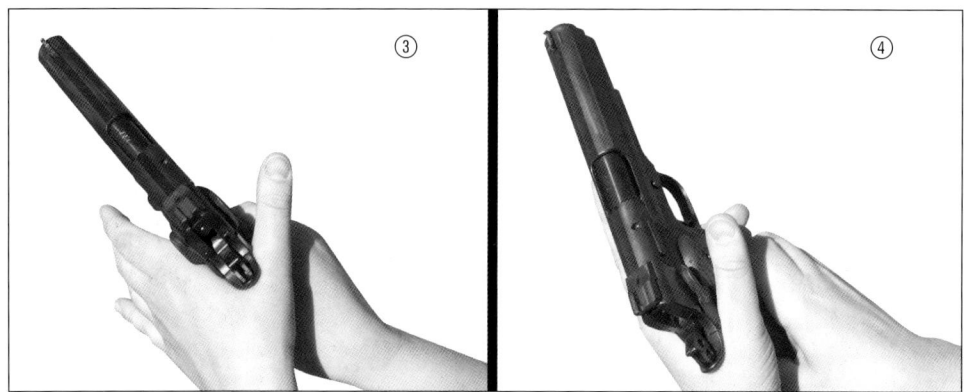

Support-Hand Transfer—Two-thirds Strong-Hand Grip

The series of photos above shows a side view of a safe and controlled strong-hand-to-support-hand transfer from the draw.

always keep the index fingers of both hands straight throughout the entire process. This usually isn't an issue with the strong hand draw, but more so with the support-hand transfer. Firing a shot during a transfer will result in disqualification from an event.

Pickups

For some stages, your gun may not be in the holster to start. It might be on a table or in a drawer or case. When picking up the gun, it is important to get a proper grip first. If at all possible, position the gun so that the gun is lying on the left side of the grip if you are right-handed and on the right side of the grip if you are left-handed. This allows your strong hand the easiest access.

Some shooters simply grasp the gun with their strong hand when picking the gun up. Others use the support hand to lift the firearm, moving the fingers of their support hand under the area near the rear sight. This allows the bottom side of the grip area to be exposed and provides easy access for the web of the strong hand to move high into the back portion of the grip.

In some divisions, like open division in USPSA, many firearms have an additional part called a slide racker. The device both allows

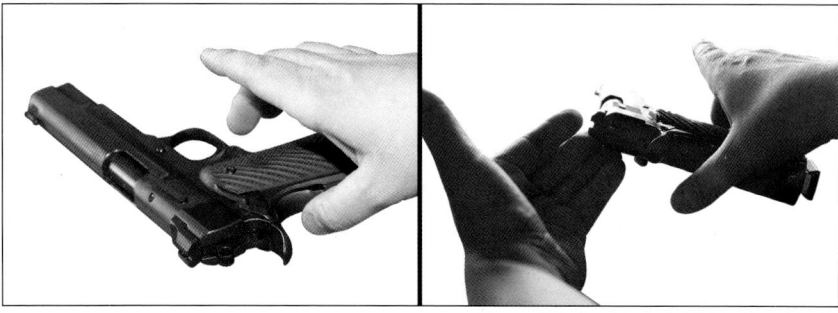

There are two common ways to pick up a handgun from a table. In the first photo, the shooter simply picks up the gun with the strong hand. In the second, the shooter uses the support hand to lift the gun at the back of the slide to provide easy access to the grip for the strong hand.

the shooter to pull the slide back quickly and easily when an optic base might prevent easy access to the slide, as well as serving as a "kickstand." When laid on its side, the slide racker places the gun in an ideal position to grasp it quickly.

> **TIP:** *For semiautos, practice pickups in dry fire with an empty magazine. If your firearm has an extended magazine release button, you might inadvertently depress the button during a pickup. If this happens, you may need to replace the button or adjust the way you grab the gun.*

The Draw & Kneeling, Squatting, and Prone

In many courses of fire you will start from a standing position, and after the start signal you will need to move into a kneeling or squatting position. In these cases, perform the same technique you would for a safe, fast draw, but incorporate movement. The best way to do this is to get a good grip on the gun, start your draw, and then begin moving your body into the squatting or kneeling position right at the moment your gun has left your holster. Delaying your full body movement slightly can help eliminate any issues where your holster could cant or tilt, resulting in a slow or awkward draw.

You might ask whether it is better to shoot from kneeling or squatting. Sometimes you may not have a choice. IDPA rules require that at least one knee be on the ground when shooting from "low cover." In other action shooting sports you can choose whether you want to squat or kneel, and there are benefits to both. The kneeling position is more stable and is desirable if you have difficult shots or the port to shoot from is very low. You may also want to shoot from kneeling in the case that it is the final position in a stage. Squatting is often preferred when shots aren't too difficult and you need to move on to another position within the course of fire. The position is less stable, but can be faster to get in and out of. Let the difficulty of the target array and the height of the port dictate what's best for you in each situation.

There are two fast ways to go prone. As described with kneeling or squatting, the first step is getting the gun out of the holster. Instead of the support hand moving to the chest, this hand moves to waist level, with the palm toward the ground. You'll use this hand to help ease you into position. If you can easily support your weight with your upper body, consider option one. If you aren't comfortable with supporting your entire weight on one arm, especially with a handgun in the other hand, use option two.

In option one, once the gun is out and pointed in a safe direction, begin to move toward the ground, kicking your feet out from under you. Use your support hand to slow your falling motion and ease yourself down into the prone position. As you lower yourself to the ground, extend your shooting hand out in front of you. You can even slide

When shooting from low positions, shooters can kneel or squat depending on target difficulty and what is comfortable for them. Keep in mind that some sports, like IDPA, require one knee on the ground while shooting from this type of position.

the base or butt of the gun along the ground. Once you're fully prone, your support hand moves up to acquire a proper grip on the pistol.

The second option requires less upper body strength. As you draw the gun from the holster, drop to your knees. Use your support hand to slow your forward movement onto the ground. Extend the shooting hand out in front of you as described above, and at the same time push your legs out so that you are completely prone. Move the support hand into place for a proper grip.

When shooting from prone, try to achieve a position that allows you to rest the butt of the gun fully on the ground. This is the most stable way to fire from the position. It allows you to take

Getting into the prone position quickly and safely involves drawing the firearm and then lowering yourself to the ground.

advantage of the ground as a very stable platform and provides the best opportunity for the fastest shot-to-shot recovery.

> 🎯 **TIP:** *When shooting from prone, you may need to adjust your position to accommodate your body type. Rollover prone is a term used to describe the shooter rolling over slightly to their strong side, as shown in this photo above of multi-world and national champion Jerry Miculek. This type of prone can help the shooter control recoil and improve accuracy by helping them achieve a proper sight picture.*

Reloading

The procedure for reloading semiautomatic pistols and revolvers differs. Regardless of the type of firearm, the first step in a successful reload begins with taking the finger off the trigger and placing it outside the trigger guard. Your finger must stay out of the trigger guard and off the trigger at all times during your reload. You will also need to make sure you pay special attention to your muzzle direction and always keep the muzzle pointed in a safe direction.

When reloading a semiauto, you must first activate the magazine release button. Depending on your firearm, this could be located on either the right or left side of the gun or even under the trigger guard. Some firearms simply use a button as a magazine release that is easily accessed with the strong-hand thumb. Others require you to push down on a lever under the trigger guard. Ideally, you want to be able to activate the magazine release with your strong hand. You can certainly use your support hand to do this, especially if you have very small hands, but it won't be as quick as doing it with just the strong hand. This is because, as you are depressing the magazine release button with your strong hand, your support hand should move down onto your belt to grab a fresh magazine.

Once the magazine clears the bottom of the gun, bend the strong-arm elbow and bring the gun in toward your body so that it is at the upper chest level. The ideal distance away from your body depends on arm length but should be between 1 and 2 feet away. Tilt the gun in your hand so that you can just see inside the magazine well.

> **LINGO:** *Magazines are commonly referred to as "mags" by shooters. Mags are often incorrectly called "clips." Clips are devices that store multiple rounds to be inserted into a magazine or cylinder.*

At the same time, the support hand is grabbing the new magazine. How you grasp this mag is critical to how fast and consistently you will be able to reload. Your magazines should be placed in magazine pouches so that the base of the magazine rests in the palm of the hand and so that the index finger of the support hand can be placed along the length of the front of the magazine. The index finger serves as a guide and allows you to feed the magazine directly into the mag well.

Once the mag is initially inserted, move the index finger out of the way and continue to push the mag into place. Depending on your firearm and how many rounds you have loaded into the magazine, it may be difficult to seat the magazine. The magazine release button needs to catch on a hole or notched area on the magazine in order to ensure that it stays in the gun. You can often hear it click or snap into place. If the magazine isn't inserted all the way, the mag can drop on the ground as you extend on target, or not feed ammunition properly. You may need to apply extra force on the base of the mag. Once the magazine is fully seated, slide your support hand into the proper grip position and extend the gun on target.

One way semiauto shooters can lose time in a reload is that, instead of keeping the gun at the upper chest level, they bring it down low near their belly area to perform the reload. In order to see the inside the mag well, the shooter has to look down instead of being able to keep their head up. I refer to this as "burying the head in the gun." If the shooter is moving during the reload, this can result in inefficient movement and a poor setup into the next position. The shooter also has to move the gun that much farther in

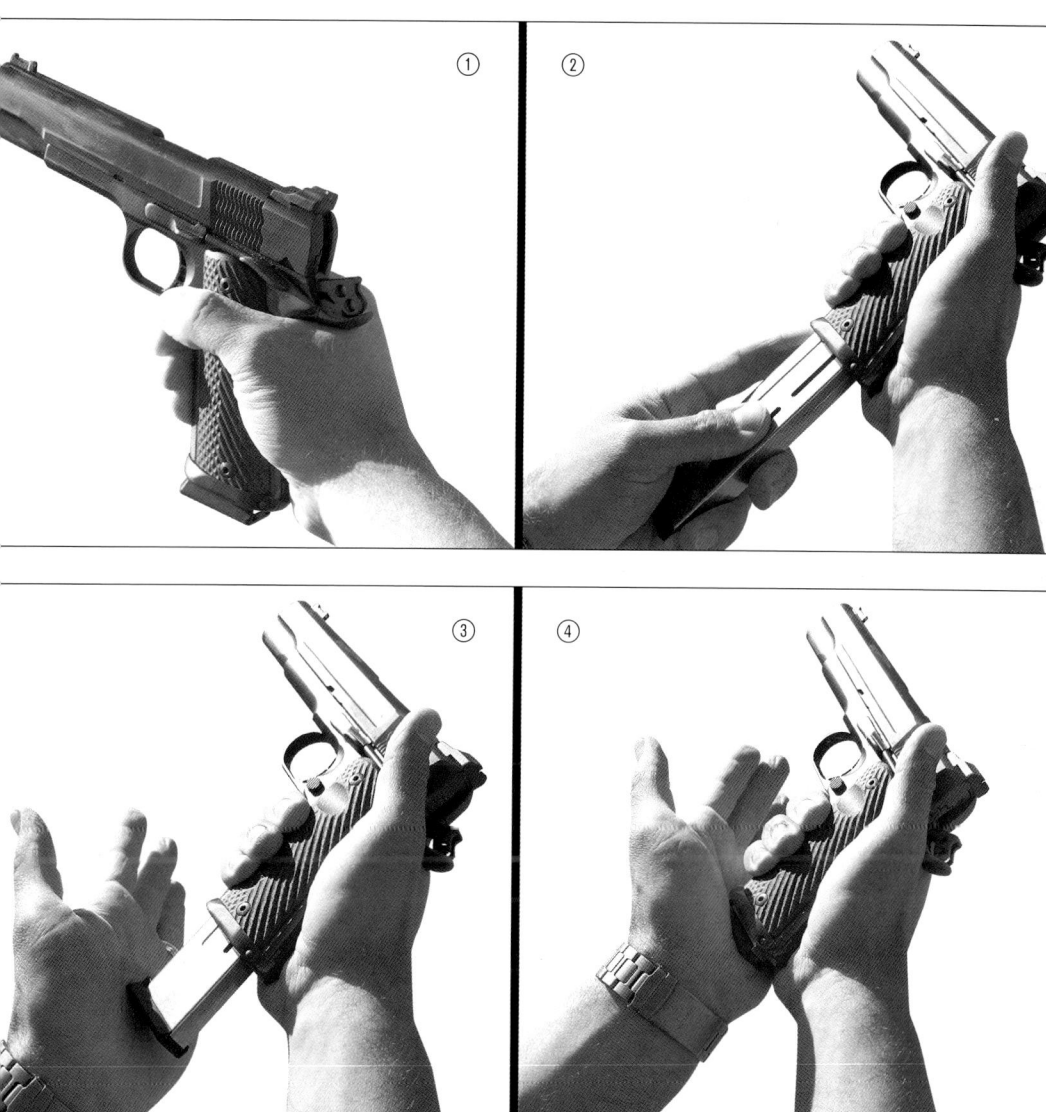

Reloading, as shown in the series of images above, is a skill that is often tested in action shooting competitions. A fast reload is efficient, with no wasted movement.

order to present it back on target. Keeping the gun high and close enough to reload efficiently allows for the most control, enables the shooter to see the magazine go into the gun, and also to present to the target faster.

The following series of images shows how looking for the mag well and keeping the gun high results in a fast, efficient reload.

Reloading with a revolver is a little bit different, and there are two popular methods. The first treats the revolver as you would a semiauto, with the gun remaining in the strong hand. The strong-hand thumb pushes forward on the cylinder release. The fingers of the support hand push the cylinder through the frame. The strong hand maintains control of the gun at all times. Next the shooter pushes the cylinder ejector rod with the support hand to eject all the empty cases, and then moves to the belt to retrieve the speed loader

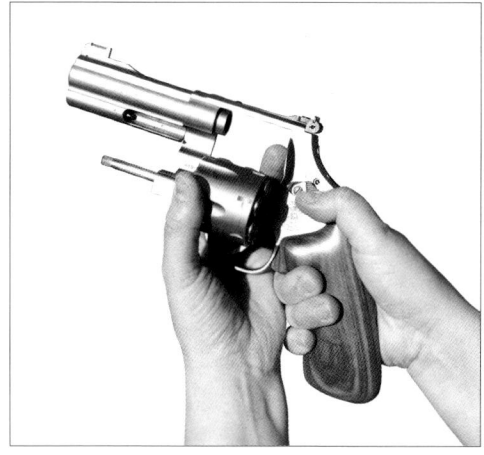

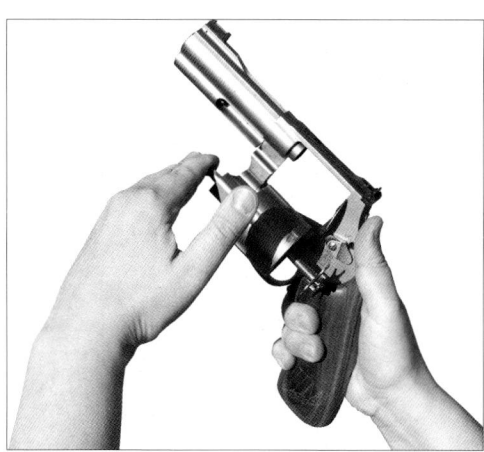

One way to reload a revolver quickly involves keeping the revolver in the strong hand at all times and loading the moon clip or speed loader into the cylinder with the support hand.

Advanced Skills >> 209

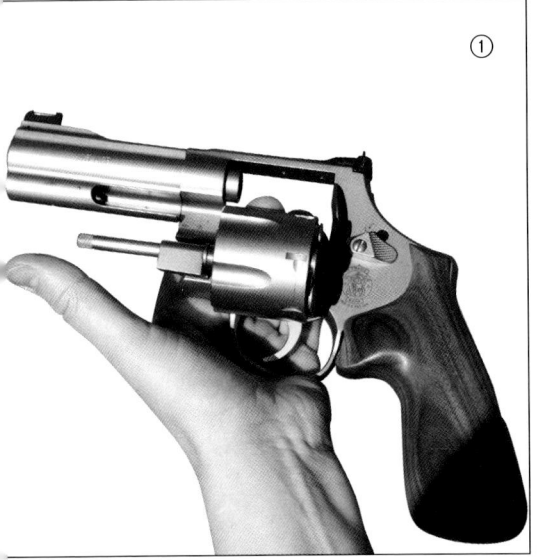
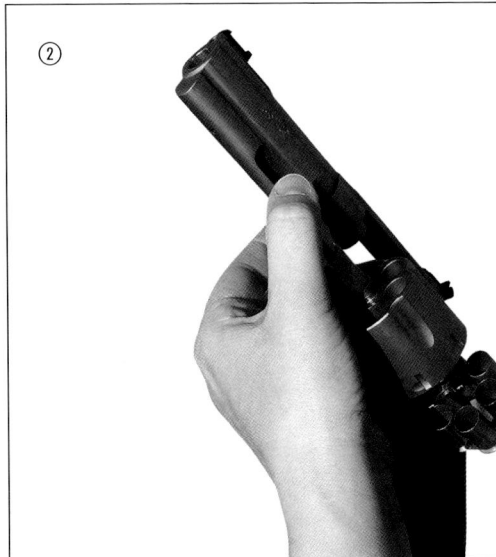
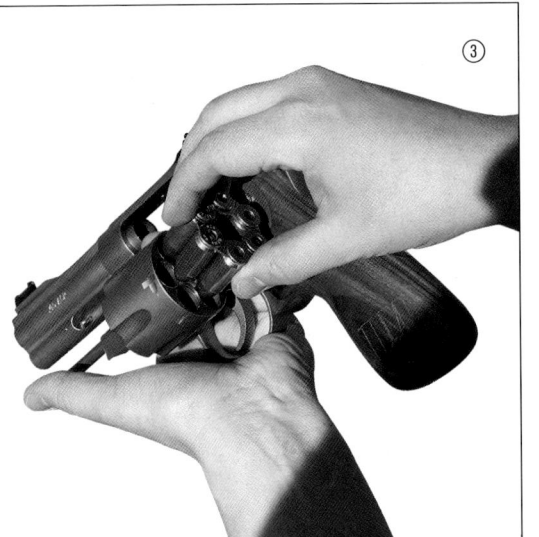
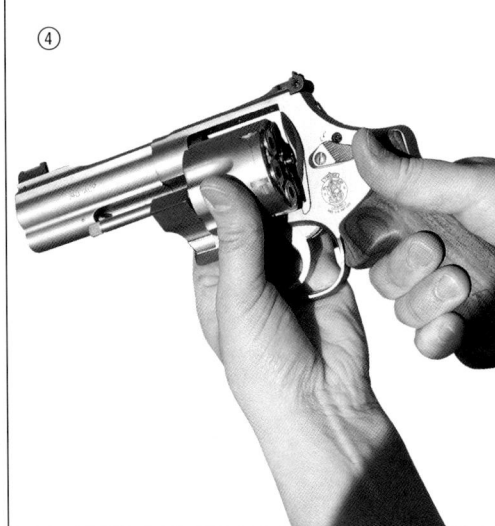

Jerry Miculek, the fastest revolver shooter in the world, reloads his revolver by transferring the firearm to his support hand and loading the cylinder with his strong hand in the same manner as pictured above.

or moon clip. The next step is to drop the cartridges into the cylinder and, if using speed loaders, remove the speed loader, letting it fall to the ground. The shooter closes the cylinder and acquires a grip with the support hand and extends out on target.

The other method to reload a revolver is often preferred by those who shoot primarily revolver competitions. Jerry Miculek, the fastest revolver shooter (and reloader) in the world, prefers this method. The main difference is that the gun is transferred to the support hand, and the strong hand is used to load the ammunition into the cylinder.

As with the first method, this reload begins with pushing forward on the cylinder release with the strong hand and using the support hand to open the cylinder. The support hand maintains control of the revolver. The shooter uses the support-hand thumb to push the cylinder ejector rod, while the strong hand releases its grip on the gun and moves to the belt. As with all reloads, it is important to be aware of muzzle direction at all times, and this type of reload is particularly susceptible to having the muzzle point back past the shooter when pushing the ejector rod to release the spent brass.

Once all the cases are clear, the support hand tilts the gun so that the openings, or chambers, in the cylinder are easily seen. The strong hand deposits the ammo into the cylinder and removes the speed loader if necessary. The shooter moves the strong hand onto the grip and uses the support hand to close the cylinder before extending out onto the target to shoot.

LINGO: *It can be confusing, but reloading is a term that is used for both magazine or clip/loader changes and is also a term used for making ammunition.*

Target Transitions

Another skill that makes the action shooting sports dynamic is requiring multiple shots on multiple targets. Even if target order is dictated, being able to transition to a target quickly is a valuable skill. For fast target-to-target transitions, it's best to position your arms in a way that your elbows are bent and flexible. Extend your arms out in front of you as if you were holding a handgun in the Isosceles Position. Now, lock your elbows so that your arms are completely straight. Move your imaginary gun from left to right as fast as you can. Now bend your arms slightly and do the same. You'll notice that you can move your arms faster with your arms bent. You also have a broader range of motion by bending the leading elbow at the extreme left and right of the movement.

In the event you have to move the gun onto another target, once you fire your final shot on the first target, you ideally want your eyes to travel to the next target first. Your eyes only have to move slightly when compared to your arms. Move your handgun to meet your line of sight and then acquire proper sight picture. Your eyes serve as a guide and allow you to get on target faster.

> **TIP:** *In the case where you have two targets stacked, a low target and a high target, start with the low target first. Use the recoil of the firearm to propel your sight picture onto the upper target for a faster transition.*

Shooting on the Move

Some people find shooting on the move to be very intimidating. The key to successfully shooting targets while moving is to move and shoot only as fast as you can see and control your sight picture on the target(s). Just as competitors in precision sports have to accept that they have an arc of movement, shooting on the move is a skill that is best executed when the shooter accepts that there will be movement in the sight picture. How the shooter moves, specifically the way they step, can greatly reduce how much the sights move on target.

Keeping the knees bent and rolling the feet softly can help you shoot targets on the move quickly and accurately.

To learn how to shoot on the move, stand completely erect, holding your arms out in front of you as if you were shooting a handgun. Begin to move forward, maintaining a good sight picture on a defined target in front of you. With each step, you should notice the sights move up and down. Depending on how heavy-footed you are, this might even have a jarring effect on your sight picture. Now bend your knees and focus on a heel-to-toe rolling motion with your steps. Your sight picture should now be more stable on the target, with less vertical movement. Walking stiffly you'll see a lot of bounce in your sight picture, but by rolling heel to toe and keeping your knees bent you'll be able to control your sights much more effectively.

> **TIP:** *When backing away from a target, keep the knees bent but move the feet toe to heel. When moving laterally on a range, use heel-to-toe motion but, depending on the direction of travel, use crossover steps by crossing over or behind the opposite foot as you step in whatever way allows you to move comfortably and efficiently without too much twist in your upper body.*

Entering Shooting Positions

In a course of fire you will likely have to move in and out of various positions. For some positions it might be a matter of taking a few steps, where others may require you to move a long distance. Look for the quickest way to travel and use the least amount of movement.

For stages requiring a lot of distance to move, move as fast as you can, but you want to be able to glide into position with the gun up and ready to shoot. The last five to 10 feet before a position is where you should start reducing your speed by taking quicker, smaller steps. Your last step into the position should ideally be with your lead foot. If you are moving left to right, this would be your right foot, and for right to left, your left foot. The gun should be up and ready to extend

When moving into a position, try to move in with the foot that is closer to the final position, called the lead foot.

out on target as you step into position, and as you move your trailing foot into a good stance, you should be ready to shoot.

You may find that a shooting position requires you to shoot from around a wall or barricade or through a window. In some cases you will need to get close to a barricade or get into a window, especially if targets are obscured, but generally when moving into these positions, it's best to stay as far back from the barricade or wall as possible. By keeping back, you can make it easier to see and engage targets. Getting too close or crowding a barrier can result in having to bring your gun in close to your body and then extend out, instead of being ready to shoot the moment you arrive. In the case with engaging targets through windows or ports, putting your gun through the opening instead of staying back will result in a slower

When shooting around barriers or through ports, it's best to keep distance between you and the barrier and also not push your gun through a port whenever possible. This allows you quick and efficient presentation onto targets and ease of moving on to the next position. Photo by Scott Carnahan.

time, as it forces you to bring your gun back out when moving on to the next position.

Moving Targets

In action shooting events, it's very common to see a wide variety of reactionary targets. In addition to falling steel, you'll often see swinging, dropping, spinning, and appearing and disappearing targets. New competitors often find these types of targets to be intimidating, especially when they move quickly. The best way to tackle a moving target is to be patient and trust your sights. Place your sights where you know the target will appear. As the target moves into position behind your sights, take the shot(s). As a general rule of thumb, it's best to try to shoot a moving target as it moves in behind your sights. If you shoot at the moving target as it leaves, moving out of your sight picture, it could move out of position as you fire, resulting in a poor hit or even a miss.

Especially for new shooters, it's best to shoot moving targets based on your personal ability level. Some competitors may be able to take two shots on a moving target before it disappears. Others may be able to shoot only one shot and must wait for the target to repeat its movement cycle and reappear. As you improve and gain experience, these types of targets will become easier for you.

LINGO: *Swingers, drop turners, sliders, bear traps, clam shells, Texas stars, whirlygigs, and max traps are all types of moving targets used in action shooting competitions.*

Breaking Down a Stage

The best competitors know the limitations of their ability, and break down a stage in a way that is fast, efficient, and plays up their strengths. Only with experience and practice will you know the best way to tackle a stage, but you can start by following this simple stage breakdown plan.

- Know your targets: Make note of the total number of rounds on the course, and account for all the targets. Look for potentially challenging targets or ones that you know you will want to plan extra time or ammunition for.
- Take into account your magazine or cylinder capacity when considering what targets to shoot from what position. It's usually best not to perform a stationary reload on a stage if you can choreograph your movement to accommodate all shots and reload on the move.
- Make a note of what targets you can see from various positions throughout the course. Some positions might provide an easier shot, but if you can reduce the number of reloads or eliminate a standing reload, it will most likely be more efficient.
- Once you have decided what targets to engage from where, consider how you will engage them. Is it faster for you to shoot from near to far, far to near, right to left, or left to right?
- If you have moving targets, note how they are activated and how long it takes them to begin to move. You may be able to engage one or more targets while waiting for the moving target to appear.
- Plan your steps and choreograph your movements from position to position. Look for the shortest distance to move, and think about how you want to both enter and exit positions.

In some sports, including IDPA, you are not allowed to physically rehearse the stage and can only decide on a plan in your mind. In other sports, you are given time to walk through the stage as a squad and plan and rehearse the stage freely. If this is the case, use the full designated walkthrough time to plan how you will tackle the stage.

Once the squad begins to shoot and competitor order is established, you can continue to prep for your turn at the stage. When you are the on-deck shooter, mentally visualize your plan while the shooter ahead of you in the order completes his or her stage. As soon as the line is called safe, move up and work through your plan. This way, when you are called to the line you are as ready as you can be to shoot. Even in sports like IDPA, where you are not allowed choreograph your movement throughout the course, you can still think through your strategy before it is your turn to shoot.

> **TIP:** *Does your stage plan have you ending on a difficult shot or a steel target? Shooters often pull off target before completing their last shot in an array. This can result in missing the target. If you plan to shoot a challenging shot as your final shot in an array, make sure you watch your sights and focus on good trigger control.*

Visualize and be flexible. Some stages have a high disaster factor, like extremely challenging targets or requiring a limited number of rounds to shoot specific targets. Think of contingency plans and the worst-case scenario for stages like these. This way, if for some reason your plan doesn't go well, you can then apply your backup to make the best of the situation.

Proper Range Etiquette

Range etiquette is certainly not mandated in shooting as it is in sports like golf, but I consider it something that all competitors should be aware of. It isn't often that shooters in action shooting find themselves online with other shooters at the same time. When it does happen, though, be courteous of your fellow competitors and try not to distract them. You should also be prepared to help out. Courses can be elaborate, especially to reset, and most action shooting matches require that participants paste targets and paint and reset steel.

Establishing a shooting order that the squad follows through the entire event can be helpful for all shooters. Easy ways to assign a shooting order include selecting an order at random for the first stage and writing it down, shooting alphabetically, or assigning the order based on a competitor number assigned by the match administration. Rotate through the order so that the first shooter on the list is the first shooter on the first stage. For the next stage, the first shooter is moved to the bottom of the list and moves up in position as the squad completes stages. Using an order also helps the squad get into a routine for both competing and resetting the stage.

Proper etiquette begins with the walkthrough. Listen to the match official issue the walkthrough in its entirety. Don't talk during the course explanation, to ensure that everyone has an opportunity to hear the procedure. You also want to show respect for the volunteers serving as match officials. If you have a question, it is best to save it for the end of the walkthrough.

If there are moving targets or intricate props that must be activated, give the courtesy to the first shooter on the stage to let him or her activate them if possible and have full view of the targets. The other shooters in the squad will have the benefit of an additional individual walkthrough time and have the opportunity to see the course in action.

> **TIP:** *Avoid swimming upstream. Shooters will file through a course during a walkthrough. Whenever possible, exit out the back of a final position to avoid interfering with other shooters as they plan their stage.*

Matches use "up," "on deck," and "in the hole" to define the shooter who is firing and those who are second and third. In most events, the shooters on deck and in the hole are allowed to arrange their gear and mentally prep for the stage. In IDPA, the up shooter stands ready to walk to the line. In USPSA, International Practical Shooting Confederation (IPSC), and Steel Challenge Shooting Association (SCSA), the shooter who is up can walk through the stage. This is the competitor's final chance to prepare and work through the stage plan. *Only* the shooter who is up should be on the course, in order to give him or her fair opportunity to prepare. All other shooters will have the same amount of time to prep on the stage. Once the shooter has completed the course, he or she should follow the scorekeeper and check and sign their score sheet; collect any magazines, moon clips, or speed loaders; and return to their bag to load up for the next stage.

The shooter on deck is waiting in the wings. This is an excellent time for the shooter to visualize and mentally rehearse their plan. Some competitors think it is acceptable for the on deck shooter to walk the stage. There is no written rule, but I disagree. Shooters who choose to walk the stage when on deck should always defer to the competitor who is up, and make extra effort to stay out of the way and allow them free rein on the course.

The shooter in the hole should use the time to make sure they have all appropriate ammunition and gear to complete the stage. They can also use this time to mentally prepare. All other shooters should help reset the stage by pasting targets, resetting steel, and moving targets and ensuring the course is ready for the next competitor.

After you're done with the stage, be sure to thank your range officers. Range officers are volunteers. I like to thank each range officer individually and shake their hands. Without their hard work and dedication, there simply wouldn't be any competitions to shoot.

Dos and Don'ts

What happens if you are disqualified from an event? Disqualifications are dreaded and can be difficult for shooters. Competitors can become embarrassed or even filled with shame for making an error, especially one that is unsafe on the range. Here are some dos and don'ts in the event that you are disqualified from a match.

> **LINGO:** *Shooters often shorten the term disqualification and refer to it as a "DQ."*

Do . . .

- Ask what you did wrong.
- Make sure you understand how and why you violated the rule(s).
- Check the rule book and verify the specific rule(s).
- Ensure that the date, time, and details of the violation are written on your score sheet.
- Offer to help finish working with your squad, at least until they finish the stage.

Don't . . .

- Make a scene or lose your temper.
- Assume that you can get out of the disqualification.
- Delay or hold up the match unnecessarily.
- Make it difficult for the rest of your squad mates to compete.

If you feel that you have been wrongly disqualified and/or the range official has not acted appropriately, ask for the range master or match director. There are specific rules that pertain to disqualifications. You may be able to file a protest for some DQ offenses.

Chapter 14 »

PRACTICE ON THE RANGE

In order to get the most out of your range time, you should have a specific set of skills and a goal to work on. Sure, you can go to the range and just shoot, but without a goal, you limit your ability to learn and improve faster. Having a goal makes your practice sessions more productive. Let's face it, shooting sports are not inexpensive. Many require not only the investment in a firearm, but additional specialized gear. Ammunition can be expensive. Ideally you want to make every single round you shoot downrange count.

For clay target shooting sports, one way to save money in practice is to purchase a hand thrower. You'll need a range buddy to throw targets for you, making sure they are thrown in a safe direction. With just the cost of buying clay targets, this can be a great way to practice acquiring the moving clays, firing the shot, and executing follow through with a shotgun.

One way to practice shooting is to look for public shooting ranges in your area. Some public ranges have specific rules that may prevent you from practicing certain skills, like drawing from a holster, for example. You also may have the option to join a private range or club to practice. Many clubs offer their members access to target systems, props, and steel targets. This isn't always an option for many shooters, though. Some clubs or ranges may not have the equipment necessary to train for specific sports. If this is the case for you, then you not only have to bring all your shooting gear, but all your targets and additional props with you.

Investing in range equipment can add to the cost of shooting. If you shoot in a single target sport, your investment can be as little as one target stand. Several companies offer steel target stands that fit wooden supports that you can easily find at home improvement stores and replace as needed.

If you compete in an action shooting sport, you'll want to invest in a number of target stands. If you're handy you can create your own using short lengths of 2 x 4 lumber attached with screws to form a stand. You can also create your own props like barricades, walls, and low walls with windows. These are pretty significant pieces of range equipment to haul to the range. You may not be able to travel around with a barricade in your car, so for some this isn't an option.

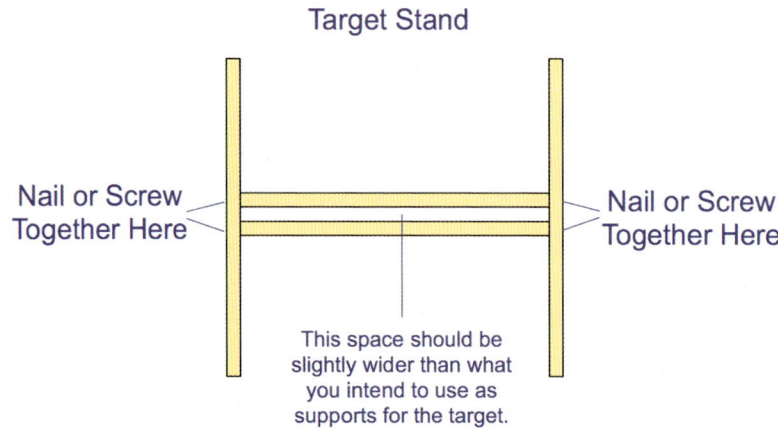

An 8-foot 2 x 4 cut into 4 pieces and screwed together makes an effective and inexpensive target stand to take to the range.

If you don't have access to these types of props, it's time to get creative. Purchasing or making a few more target stands can help you create a wide variety of props. A target stand using a piece of cardboard from a box can be used as both a barricade and a low port. Put a staple gun and more cardboard to work, and you can create a wall of cardboard with ports to shoot through. Watch videos on the Internet for prop inspiration to create a wide variety of shooting positions that will challenge your skills—things like shooting from around the left and right sides of barricades, through low ports, and around vision barriers. Use rocks or sandbags to keep your walls and barricades from blowing over in windy conditions. The advantage of using target stands and cardboard to create your props is that you can change them frequently. Wooden versions of the same things can limit you by presenting the same challenge over and over again.

USPSA and IDPA shooters often feel that they have to set up complete courses of fire in order to reap the benefits of training. You can set up what I call mini-courses that test one or two skills. Use props to create small stages with just one or two positions. Save the long field courses for matches. You can still work the skills—it's just a matter of piecing them all together to use in one stage in actual competition. Setting up smaller courses also makes limited training time more productive. You can spend more time shooting and less time resetting.

Targets are another expendable item for shooters to invest in. Each sport has an official target that can be purchased through specific target suppliers. Buying targets in bulk helps you reduce your cost. Another solution is to simply make your own.

For many precision sports, it's easy to make your own targets. If you have a target stand, use cardboard from a box to make a backer. Next, make your own bull's-eye target on a piece of white copy paper. Don't worry about each scoring ring. A simple black circle will do. Then make copies of your target using a copy machine. The idea is to get used to aiming for a specific size target. You won't be able to score your target as you would in a match, but by shooting on a target like this, your goal is to hit as close to the center as many times as possible. Sometimes people get wrapped up in their scores on a target without looking at how they actually shot. Using black dot targets like this will help you focus on your shooting, not your score, in practice.

For some precision sports, targets are just too large to practically make your own. For precision rifle events, you also may be limited in how far you can shoot in practice. For events like these, consider making your own reduced target. Create a target that mimics the size of what the target looks like at distance but is at a closer range. The point is to improve your accuracy skills. Reduced-size, close-range targets may not help you train properly for reading the wind or the mirage. Train those skills whenever possible on suitable ranges, and spend your available practice time to improve what you can—things like your position, trigger control, and follow through.

Steel targets can be pricey, but have a lot of training value. You may wish to invest in just one steel target to help you get used to shooting on steel. A common pitfall for many shooters is to look over the gun at reactionary steel targets instead of getting a good sight picture. A simple steel plate, one that does not fall, can provide you with both a challenging target and one that can be incorporated into a variety of courses.

A single steel target like the one pictured above offered by Action Target is portable and allows you to practice shooting on steel without having to reset it.

Steel Challenge is probably one of the most friendly of the action shooting sports for shooters to get started in. A major drawback of the course of fire, though, is that most people don't have access to enough steel targets, especially those that meet the regulations for Steel Challenge stages. It is indeed possible to train for Steel Challenge stages without steel. Simple paper plates and cardboard cutouts can do the job. There's actually even a benefit to shooting paper targets over steel targets. When shooting on steel, because you have the auditory feedback of when your bullets strike the target, you may be listening for your hits for confirmation. Working with paper only can help you to learn to trust your sight picture and engage the trigger in a way that's going to allow you to hit the target.

Bottom line, you don't have to drop lots of money on the expendable items like targets that you're going to use up in practice. A little bit of creativity can go a long way in preparing for your next competition.

Knowing Your Ability

Knowing your own shooting ability helps you maintain perspective. Is it reasonable to think that you will be able to shoot a personal best every time you compete? Should you expect that you will shoot a perfect score your first match out? No. What you can expect is to perform based on what you are capable of, constantly striving for improvement and to do your best. Try not to become disappointed with your score based on other shooters' results. Yours is the only score you can affect. Having a realistic understanding of your ability combined with a positive, optimistic attitude will help you take pride in your personal accomplishments on the range.

For the action shooting sports, because so much more is tested beyond pure shooting, knowing your ability level for each skill can help you plan how you will tackle a given course of fire. Because these sports often use challenging moving targets with activators, shooters can often feel overwhelmed. When faced with a target array with stationary, steel, and moving targets, it can be difficult to decide the best way to shoot them. Some competitors may opt to engage targets more conservatively, shooting an activator target and then waiting for a moving target to appear. Another option is to shoot moving targets like swingers at the end of a given array when their movement has slowed, making for easier shots. If a shooter is fast enough, it might be possible to shoot one or more targets before the moving target even appears.

Top shooters can tell you exactly how long it will take to shoot high-scoring hits on a target at various distances. They also know how long it takes them to transition to targets of varying degrees of difficulty across the range. The best competitors know their abilities for these skills and many more, including how fast they can sprint a distance while running with a firearm, how fast they can reload in certain conditions, and how long it takes them to move into prone and kneeling positions from standing. When presented with a course of fire, they can then apply their known times to figure out the best plan to shoot a stage.

Because every shooter is different, the only way you will learn the current limits of your ability is to practice and record your average times. One investment to consider is a timer. Shot timers record each shot fired, measuring the time in hundredths of a second. Most shot timers have the capability to delay the start signal so that you can operate them in training by yourself. Keeping a journal and writing down the time it takes you to shoot different targets and arrays can help you plan how to tackle stages in competitions. Keep in mind that as you improve, these times will change.

Mimicking Competition in Dry Fire

I seem to mention dry fire a lot in this book. There's a good reason. Dry fire is one of the best ways to perfect techniques. I discussed using dry fire to work on fundamental skills earlier in this book, as well as using it to develop more advanced skills. You can also dry fire to simulate competition. Remember, dry fire means absolutely *no ammunition* anywhere around you, or even in the room.

In precision sports, you may not have the opportunity to compete in matches often. Dry firing is one way to help you prepare for an event in the comfort of your own home. You can even dry fire and visualize shooting an entire match. It takes a bit of creativity, and a lot of focus with visualization skills, but you can build up your match endurance while reaping the benefits of working on your fundamentals.

For action shooting sports, you can use smaller versions of targets and set up entire courses of fire in your home. Some target suppliers offer airsoft targets that incorporate the shapes and scoring rings of standard targets but are just reduced in size. Use walls or doorways to simulate shooting from barricades. Kneel around your couch or over your ottoman to dry fire from low cover. Unless you are using a double-action firearm, you won't be able to feel the trigger squeeze for all shots unless you reset the trigger each time, but you can work on moving in and out of position and fast acquisition of the sights on target.

Another way to dry fire effectively in action shooting is to use your timer. Many timers are feature-packed, allowing you to establish par times where a buzzer sounds to signal the start and then again for the stop. For timed events like Bianchi Cup, this can be very helpful in ingraining time limits while drawing and getting into position. For speed events, you can use a par time to help push you. If your standard draw time from hands relaxed at sides is 1.5 seconds, set the par time on your timer to 1.4 seconds. You'll find that you will begin to race to get to the gun and complete your draw. Continue to lower your par times until you can no longer complete the skill.

When pushing your speed on specific skills, you may notice that your technique begins to falter. If you start to fumble or notice that you are creating bad habits like putting your finger on the trigger too soon, take away the time element and slowly work through the motions. When I dry fire specific skills, I like to start out slow and try to achieve perfection each time. Next, I open up the throttle and start pushing my speed. Toward the end of the session I go back to a fast but controlled speed, one that I would feel confident about in competition.

Cross Training

Maybe you are already a competition shooter. Perhaps you have participated in another shooting sport and hit a bit of a slump. You may consider yourself a specialist in a specific sport and even though you may be devoted to that sport, cross training in other events can help improve your performance. Cross training or competing in another event can help you learn a skill that you can then apply to your primary sport.

You can look for sports that are similar, like USPSA, Steel Challenge, and IDPA. Many of the skills tested are similar in both, but the differences can carry over to help you become well rounded. In precision sports, you might want to try a whole new division with a different type of firearm. If you compete in NRA Conventional Pistol, you might want to consider giving air pistol a try, as this sport eliminates the distraction of dealing with significant recoil.

Consider exploring sports that might be completely different. Look for competitions that incorporate and challenge your weaknesses. An example would be to take up a precision rifle sport as a multi-gun shooter, or giving Steel Challenge a try if you compete in Olympic Sport Pistol or Rapid Fire. If you compete in multi-gun but really struggle with hitting long-distance targets, picking up a precision rifle sport will help you with the ability to hit targets at long range. If you compete in rapid fire or sport pistol, where you need to fire shots quickly, trying out Steel Challenge in Rimfire Division can help you acquire your sights and build confidence for shooting fast shots. Cross training, especially during the off-season, can help take you to the next level.

Cross training can help keep you from burning out. Let's say you've been shooting for a long time, shooting the same type of competitions, with the same shooters, at the same time and place. You may have lost the desire to compete altogether. Sometimes taking a break from competition is good for your shooting. You may go cold turkey or better yet, look for ways to reinvigorate the passion for shooting. Sometimes just a simple switch or slight change in the sports and types of competitions you shoot can ignite the spark. Cross training is a great way to give your shooting a jump-start.

Airsoft

Because not everyone has access to firearms internationally, in many countries there are shooting programs that incorporate all the elements of competition with live ammunition, but use guns that fire plastic pellets. These are called airsoft guns. There are even manufacturers who customize airsoft guns to mimic the real firearms used in highly modified divisions, such as the Open Division in Steel Challenge.

Many competition shooters incorporate airsoft training into their practice. Complete courses of fire can be set up in basements or garages. For winter months, this type of training can be the next best thing to live fire. The important thing to remember with airsoft is that you make sure you understand that BBs can damage walls. Ensure that you wear suitable eye protection at all times. It's also a good idea to clear the paths of BBs where you will be walking or running to prevent slipping on the projectiles.

Rimfire

Another way to save money but still reap the benefits of good training is to shoot .22 caliber. Several companies offer conversion kits for pistols and rifles that convert these firearms from centerfire to rimfire. For those who choose to compete with the Smith & Wesson M&P series pistol and rifle, the company offers models in

.22 rimfire. The benefit of both the M&P series and the conversion kits is that these guns look and can feel the same as the full-powered versions, only with reduced recoil. It's still best to save some centerfire training ammunition to learn how to control recoil, but a combination of centerfire and rimfire training can make shooting more economical.

Whether you are an avid competitor looking to start a new sport or are someone who is completely new to shooting sports, what you practice and how you train can help you excel. A visit to your home improvement store, making your own paper targets, and exploring rimfire and/or airsoft options can also help reduce the impact on your wallet.

Chapter 15 »

FROM NEWBIE TO CHAMPION

As with any sport, in shooting if you don't dedicate time to train you cannot expect to be a champion. Some shooters have no intention of winning the next world title, and there's nothing wrong with that. These individuals enjoy competitions as a way to improve shooting skills, interact with like-minded people, and have fun. They may consider themselves weekend warriors of sorts when it comes to competing in matches. These are the shooters who represent the grassroots of competitions. Without them and the generous volunteers who dedicate their time to work events, there would be no shooting sports.

There are others who are naturally competitive and strive to be the best they can be. They want to excel, be champions within their disciplines. Regardless of whether you're just looking to improve a few skills or become the next national champion, this section will cover how you can become a better performer at matches.

In order to be successful in competition you have to have a strong set of fundamentals. These skills are your foundation and include the basics of grip, stance, sight alignment, and trigger control, as well as

In order to have a safe, fun shooting event it takes dedicated volunteers and competitors at every level, like these at the NRA Bianchi Cup, Action Pistol National Championship.

sport-specific advanced skills that are frequently tested in the heat of competition. The first step in becoming a better shooter within your sport is to know and understand your sport.

Make a list of all the skills that you have been, or will be, tested on in competition. Then rank the skills based on your ability to perform them. You can use either a detailed numbering system or categorize them using poor, good, and best, based on how you feel that you can perform each skill. This isn't easy and requires you to be completely honest with yourself. The next step is coming up with a plan that allows you to keep your good and best skills in shape but improves those that you need to work on.

Take a close look at the skills you feel are your weak areas. Ask yourself if you can improve any of these skills safely at home in dry fire. By working on your technique in dry fire, you fine-tune and isolate the skill so that when you do have the opportunity to practice with ammunition on a range, you can focus on adding live fire to the particular skill.

It's easier to work on the things we know we are good at. It's more fun. It's less work. Who wants to spend hour after hour working on something that they aren't good at? That's the real challenge, and it is critical in order to become successful in your sport.

Keep in mind that if you dedicate all your time to improving your weak areas and stop training the skills that you are good at, you may find that those "good or best" rated skills are now your weak skills. Sometimes shooters focus solely on what they're bad at, and that results in losing the ability to be good at what they're good at. The key is finding the balance, and the best way to do that is with a log.

Think of logging as your time card to improvement. The only way you can honestly know how much time and effort you have put into shooting and improving your skills is by logging it. Shooting, for the vast majority of competitors—even those who are considered to be "pros"—is really only a hobby. Most have day jobs and obligations that make training a challenge. The number of competitors who shoot for a living in comparison to those who participate is extremely low.

How can logging help you? Logging keeps everything in perspective. It allows you to track what and how you have trained, but it can also help you take pride in your accomplishments. A good logging system allows you to be your own coach. Let's say between work and family obligations you can only dedicate time to training for a total of two hours each week, and you compete in matches on the weekends. You feel that your draw from a holster is slower than it should be for someone in your classification.

You set a plan into motion where you will spend 10 minutes a day three to four times a week working on improving your draw. You are able to reserve about an hour and a half for live fire on a range. You plan to dedicate twenty full minutes to your draw in your live fire practice session, with the rest of the time addressing other shooting skills. You follow this plan for three weeks.

By logging your training for each skill practiced for a specific amount of time (in the example above, one month) you are setting a detailed goal and working toward it. If you never make a plan to work on the skills you want to improve, it isn't reasonable to expect that you will improve. Recording how you train over a period of time will help you track whether or not you have improved in either your ability to shoot better scores on targets or shoot faster, depending on your sport.

Set up a log so that you record valuable information to track your progress. You may choose to write your statistics in a journal or you may opt to log your results as you go, using your phone or personal electronic device. I prefer to write down my stats and later type them on my computer into a database program that allows me to organize the data and filter information easily. You can even create and tailor your own log using programs like Excel or Numbers. Things to include in your log:

Overall Goal—Write down the overall goal you wish to accomplish. This can be anything from winning the national championship in your sport to learning and simply exploring and enjoying a new shooting sport. Be realistic, but also challenge yourself. Writing your overall goal and reading it each time you train and compete will help keep you inspired and focused.

Session or Competition Goal(s)—Unlike your overall goal, the goals you list in this section are specific to your training session or competition. Write down what you want to accomplish. This can be just one skill or area to work on, or several. Try to stick to one to three goals in this section. Too many goals might result in not achieving any.

Date and time—This, combined with other details in your log, can help you identify trends. Perhaps you have better training sessions in the mornings. This might be the most productive time for you to work on improving your skills and can help you plan for both practice and when you shoot in competitions.

Location—I find it's helpful to include both the range or facility name as well as the city and state of where you are shooting.

Duration—This particular section can be fun to review at the end of the year. If you are entering this into a spreadsheet or database program, be consistent in how you type in this information. You can use the format of just minutes, or hours and minutes. Keeping entries consistent will help you tally totals by week, month, and year easily.

Type of shooting—Make a note of what you're shooting for each session. Perhaps you compete or cross train in other shooting sports. Your entry here can be sport-specific, like USPSA, IDPA, SCSA, etc. or generic, like clay targets, precision, action, etc.

Serial number(s) of the firearm(s) and number of rounds fired—Keeping track of the number of rounds through each firearm you use will help you keep up with recommended maintenance schedules and help you know when to replace any parts.

Practice/competition – Enter whether this was a competition or a training session.

Who you are shooting with—You may be shooting by yourself, training with a partner, or competing with friends. You may notice you shoot better or worse when shooting with some individuals. A log can help you determine whom to shoot with for future practice and competitions.

Conditions—Was it extremely hot, or very cold? Were you shooting in the rain and mud? Feeling under the weather? Make a note of it. If you don't record challenging conditions, you may have a skewed view of your performance over time. By taking them into account and how you shot in them, you can better prepare for tough conditions in the future, especially if you have to compete in them.

Breakdown—This is the meat of your log. If this is a training session, describe the skills you worked on and how long you trained each skill or drill. If this is a competition, go into detail about the event.

Competition Results—In addition to writing down your overall score, note the match, division or category winner, their score and classification, as well as the total number of people you were competing against. This helps keep things in perspective. Let's say you log two competitions. In one you shot a good score but came in last because there were 50 experienced competitors, all with higher classification ratings. In the other you shot very poorly but placed second in a small field of 10 competitors who all compete at lower classification levels. On paper just stating a second-place finish looks better than coming in 50th, but the point of the log is to track your results in a way that reflects them accurately.

Personal Bests—This is where you celebrate! Keep track of your fastest times on specific skills, best scores, and best performances. Consider creating lists of specific personal bests like fastest draws and reloads, the highest number of 10s in a string of fire, or the best score you shot in a clay target event so that you can find and update them easily.

Performance Rating—I use this section to give myself a personal evaluation on how I perform. You can use a star rating or scale yourself on a 1–10 format. This differs from posting your results in a competition, because this is how you personally feel about your performance. You may have walked away with a win or posted high in the results, but were sloppy in executing your skills. You may have had the match of your life, but didn't fare well in the results. Perhaps you were feeling under the weather, but were proud of how you followed your plan on every shot or stage. Rating your own performance can be difficult. Remember, being honest with yourself can help identify areas to improve and will make you a stronger competitor.

Things to work on—This is your to-do list of things you need to train. Dissect each performance, break down the skills, and record them for your next session.

Notes—See a new prop you want to build? Need more pasters to repair targets? Is your range going to be closed for your next planned session? This section is useful for jotting down tidbits of information to make sure you make the most of the next time you hit the range.

Positive Reflection—I strive to end each of my practice sessions on a good note. I will be honest and say that some days that is difficult! It's important to keep a positive attitude and a sense of fun when you are shooting. Because a log tends to focus on working on your weak areas, I suggest ending log entries with a positive statement or describing a particularly productive moment in your training.

⚠ *If you are training by yourself, always keep a cell phone on you. Let someone know when and where you plan to shoot. Make sure the range has a first aid kit and/or trauma kit, or even consider bringing your own with you. Bring plenty of water and appropriate clothing.*

The Mental Game

There is a wealth of information on sports psychology. Competitors might have all the skills necessary to be top performers, but lack a mental game that allows them to thrive in the heat of competition. Just as we all have different preferences for what music we like to listen to, we all handle competition and mental management differently. I have read many books on the subject in the quest to improve my mental game, and I truly believe this is the one area that no one can claim to have completely mastered. The physical skills tested might all be the same, but each competition, with its field of competitors and conditions, is unique. You will also constantly evolve as a competitor.

One challenge that new and experienced shooters all face is dealing with nerves. Despite competing for over twenty years, I still sometimes get what I refer to as "first-stage jitters." For the first course in a match, I often feel a bit overloaded with excitement and anticipation. It usually dissipates by the time I have moved on to my next stage, but dealing with this excitement can be a challenge. For new competitors, there may be nerves associated with shooting for the first time, or tension over the fact that you will be shooting in front of a group of people—not unlike giving a speech to a crowded room. This is all normal.

Having to perform on the spot is a difficult thing. Add to that the pressure of fierce competition against other shooters, and nerves can definitely come into play. Learning how to deal with your nerves

The Mover Event at the NRA Bianchi Cup is one of the most nerve-racking events in action shooting sports. Not only do competitors have the challenge of shooting at a moving target as far away as 25 yards, but also in front of a crowd of people in stands positioned behind the firing line.

is going to help you in becoming a better competitor from match to match. Having a case of the nerves is a mental condition that manifests itself with physical side effects. An elevated heart rate, shakiness, and other sensations can feel overwhelming. To counteract the physical affects, you first have to accept that it's OK to be nervous. Fighting a case of the nerves has a tendency to backfire. Instead, understand that you are excited, but try to control how you react to it. One way to do this is to take slow, deep breaths. Controlled

Man-vs.-man shoot-offs in action shooting matches represent intense match pressure. Multi-world and national champions Doug Koenig and Michael Voigt assume the start position before racing to finish their own set of steel targets before the other. The best shooters thrive in these conditions and are able to focus on their shooting instead of their competitor's.

breathing can help your heart rate return to normal. Try standing on one foot or balancing on the balls of your feet. Putting yourself in a position that requires you to balance and maintain focus can help distract you from nervous tension.

Nerves are just another form of excitement and can even help contribute to what makes competition thrilling. Battling nerves while performing is going to make any victory all the more special. You're going to remember how you felt and the exhilaration that goes with it when you accomplish your goal, probably more than you remember actually shooting your targets.

Match pressure is different from dealing with nerves. Match pressure is the combination of the shooting challenge and the element of competition. Maybe you have just one rival, or perhaps the field is deep, with many contenders. It's easy to get caught up in how others are performing, but in the end, the only performance you have control over is your own.

Some competitors don't know how to deal with match pressure. Instead of embracing competition, they flee from it, looking for ways to avoid competing with the top contenders in their field or classification. This only showcases a weakness in their mental game. Dodging the competition can cause you to be completely unprepared and inexperienced when dealing with match pressure. Thrown into a situation where you must compete in those conditions, you have little experience with how to handle the pressure successfully. The best way to learn how to deal with match pressure is to put yourself in it as much as possible. The more you expose yourself to top competition, the better you will be prepared for when you find yourself in a heated battle for the win. Match pressure is not a bad thing, and when you solve your personal equation for how to deal with it, the result is rewarding and the experience you gain invaluable.

Another way to improve your mental game is to come up with a consistent system and plan for preparing for events. Create checklists that help you pack everything you need for a competition. Figure out what makes you feel most confident. Some shooters keep a journal or listen to music to help them focus or relax. Try to replicate your preparation process as much as possible. This includes things like setting up your gear, loading your magazines or moon clips, and when and how you visualize your next shot or stage.

Attitude

"Nothing can stop the man with the right mental attitude from achieving his goal; nothing on earth can help the man with the wrong mental attitude."

—Thomas Jefferson

This is the mushy, feel-good section of the book that is often not associated, at least in stereotypes, with extreme sports—and yes, many consider shooting to be "extreme." At the very least, consider the benefits of a positive attitude over a negative one.

A bad attitude at a match means that you are probably not having a good time. The weather may be poor, the match might be running slow, you may have shot a bad shot or run a course poorly. All those negative things add up, but add a bad attitude to the mix and you can guarantee you won't have a good time. Chances are you can ruin it for others as well.

Those who show up to the range with a good attitude truly enjoy shooting. Whether they have a good performance or a bad one, those with a positive attitude are going to have fun. A positive attitude, a smile, and an understanding that you did the best you could do at that given moment are going to help you enjoy the journey all the more. Shooters who become angry easily may find that they are their own worst enemies.

Some might think that a happy-go-lucky attitude means that you don't care, especially when you don't perform well. That's simply not true. It is perfectly fine to be upset with a poor performance, but the way you deal with it affects how long you deal with it. Take the time to reflect and make any adjustments necessary, but move on. Don't be too hard on yourself, and don't pass your unhappiness on to others. Negativity breeds more negativity. A positive attitude helps you build the mental base to become successful.

Physical Factors

Being physically fit is a benefit in the shooting sports. Even in precision events where the point is to control all movement, being fit can help you become a top performer. Upper body strength improves your ability to hold and reduce your arc of movement. Those in better shape often have a lower heart rate and can stand the rigors of intense conditions on the range.

In the action shooting sports, speed and agility are both tested. Some events are more physical than others, but even in the NRA Bianchi Cup, the most precision-intense action shooting sport, the ability to be able to get into the prone position quickly is a great benefit. In IDPA competitions, it is common to have to move, lift, or carry props to a position or even hold them while shooting. In multi-gun, not only do competitors have to haul guns and ammo with them on stages while they compete, they have to move all their equipment from stage to stage in an event.

Being physically fit gives a shooter an advantage in action shooting sports. In the match pictured above, competitors were required to lean using only a rope for support while engaging targets with one hand.

Another way to ensure you have the opportunity to do your best is to make sure you are drinking and eating properly. Staying hydrated can become a factor on both indoor and outdoor ranges. Outside, shooters face the elements like heat, humidity, cold, and

From Newbie to Champion » **247**

wind. It is easy to become dehydrated. Indoor ranges can have the same effect. Ventilation and exhaust systems that keep lead levels safe also suck the moisture out of the air, making very dry conditions.

If you become dehydrated you may feel weak and shaky. You may not feel as strong and not only can it affect you physically, but it can be detrimental to your confidence. You may not even know that you're dehydrated until it's too late. The best course of action is to drink constantly throughout the competition or training. Be prepared to bring your own water with you to an event in case there isn't any available for sale.

Food is another area that people can overlook. Perhaps you are used to eating three square meals a day. A long day on the range can burn a lot of calories, from actual competition to nervous energy. Some competitors don't like to eat, especially if they are concerned with dealing with match nerves. They fear that eating anything will upset their stomachs and make it difficult to shoot well.

Use smaller events to learn what kinds of foods will give you the energy you need to maintain a certain level of performance so that you can eat without issue. It's best if it is something that you can easily find and purchase when on the road. A common problem for athletes who travel all over the world to compete is that it might be difficult to find these items in the local grocery store abroad. You may want to consider bringing food with you to provide a level of consistency and a sense of comfort.

> **TIP:** *Eat like an athlete at the range. Snacking on fruits, nuts, and healthy energy bars can help keep you energized throughout a match. Avoid greasy, heavy foods as well as those with refined sugars like those found in candy and soda.*

Finally, show up prepared. Make sure you clean and inspect your equipment to ensure everything is serviceable and in working order and that it meets the rule requirements of your sport. Dealing with gear issues in a competition can be stressful and can have a negative impact on your mental game. You want to show up to each event prepared so that the only thing you need to focus on is your performance.

Whether you are a seasoned competitor looking to improve your game or someone who has never fired a gun before, I hope you reap the benefits of learning to handle firearms safely as you participate in shooting sports and most of all, feel a sense of accomplishment as you evolve as a shooter. Be safe and have fun!